DEDICATION

This book is dedicated in the memory of
my father, Isadore Kramer, who gave me
a love of learning and to Dr. Erbert F.
Cicenia, who provided the professional
opportunity to learn and grow.

SEXUALITY and the MENTALLY RETARDED

A Clinical and Therapeutic Guidebook

by Rosalyn Kramer Monat, M.Ed., CCC-SLP

AASECT Certified Sex Educator/Sex Counselor

COLLEGE-HILL PRESS
SAN DIEGO

Cover photograph by George N. Connor

College-Hill Press, Inc.
4580-E Alvarado Canyon Road
San Diego, California 92120

Library of Congress Cataloging in Publication Data

Monat, Rosalyn Kramer
  Sexuality and the mentally retarded.
  1. Sex instruction for the mentally handicapped.   2. Mentally handicapped —
  Sexual behavior.

I. Title. [DNLM: 1. Education of mentally retarded. 2. Counseling.
  3. Sex education. LC 4601 M736s]
HQ54.3.M66 1982   613.9'5'0880826   82-9647

ISBN 0-933014-75-9

Printed in the United States of America

CONTENTS

FOREWORD

For the past ten years I have been concentrating my efforts on improving the social-sexual aspects of rehabilitation programs for mentally handicapped persons. In this short period of time it has been an exhilarating experience for me to witness a new body of knowledge develop, from literally nothing, to dozens of books, journal articles, curricula, and audio-visual materials directly relating to the sexuality of persons who have disabilities that hinder their learning.

In the early seventies a mere handful of us lectured, taught, and trained other professionals with similar interests and goals. The results of our efforts are now a pyramidal network of experts spread throughout the U.S., Canada, Europe, and such far away places as Australia, Singapore, and Hong Kong. It has been gratifying to see how professionals, such as the author of this book, responded to these early contacts, assuming leadership roles as advocates of the social-sexual rights of the mentally handicapped.

Ms. Monat was one of my own outstanding trainees who eagerly integrated what information I was able to give her. She, in turn, effectively trained her colleagues and established counseling and sex education programs for clients and parents. Her writings are a fine example of the important role that first hand experiences have played in the establishment of this new field of endeavor.

The book should serve its readers well. To me, its special value is the author's rich use of case histories to exemplify and clarify the points she provides us. Ms. Monat should be congratulated for filling another important niche in our growing knowledge about the too long neglected subject of the sexuality of mentally retarded persons.

Winifred Kempton
M.S.W., ACSW
International Consultant
on Social Behavior of
the Mentally Retarded

PREFACE

"If it's a boy, I'll name him Johnny. If it's a girl I'll name her Jill. Oh, it doesn't matter — Just as long as it's normal. Oh, a boy — six pounds. Is he O.K.? — ten fingers, ten toes, penis, and all that — O.K. — I guess that's over. Let's watch Johnny grow up. Before you know it, he'll go to college. Retarded — what's retarded? He's my child. He can't be —."

These are some of the familiar and common thoughts of all people who have ventured into the realm of parenthood. Producing a baby with problems is something that always happens to the "other person." When it happens to one's self, the whole situation seems to be unrealistic and takes a great deal of time before the parent can adjust to the fact that this "horrible" situation is actually happening.

The adjustment to having a handicapped child is difficult in itself. To further understand that this handicapped child has problems in learning and is mentally retarded is even harder to accept. To then go one step further and realize that this handicapped individual has personality areas that develop the same as normal children, is almost impossible to accept.

When one comes right down to it, acknowledging the existence of and development of sexuality in a child who is handicapped is extremely difficult for the parent and society. There is a great tendency on the part of the parent and society to infantalize the retarded individual, regardless of chronological age. Included in this infantalization is the concept of asexuality, or lack of sexuality, which extends to the lack of necessity for learning about one's self, one's sexuality, or one's psychosexual development. Therefore, as they go through the process of maturation, many mentally retarded individuals find themselves in a position where no one in their environment is willing to deal with or even recognize their developing sexuality.

In institutions for the retarded, community programs for the retarded, etc., the subject of sexuality seems to be a very threatening, taboo topic. Staff and administrators approach the area as if it is one that would automatically cause problems. It is the hope of most parents and administrators that, in the area of sexuality and the mentally retarded, everything will be just "O.K." and not have to be handled or discussed.

As I have developed my skills in the field of sex counseling with the mentally retarded, I have been through many processes beneficial to others in the field who are dealing with sexuality and the mentally retarded. This book is written as a tribute to the mentally retarded who have enabled me to gain this knowledge of their sexuality. I hope that it will be an aid to those parents, administrators, educators, and programmers in gaining the necessary skills and abilities needed to acept the feelings of mentally retarded individuals so that they, in turn, understand their own developing sexuality. I feel that it is the right of the mentally retarded to have this acknowledgment, help, and support.

This book is not a technical or research adventure. Neither is it designed to incorporate all the present research into one volume. I have found that there is a need for a sharing of experiences and knowledge from a very pragmatic point of view. I offer suggestions, not solutions — techniques that have been tried, some with success, some with failure. There is a need for thoughts and a willingness to examine the field. To all those involved with the mentally retarded, I say that these individuals have the right to express and develop their own sexuality and to feel comfortable with it. I believe it is the responsibility of everyone in the environment of these individuals to acknowledge, recognize, and offer support systems for the mentally retarded so they can control this aspect of their personality development and maturation. We need to acknowledge that the sexuality of the retarded is as important as the development of adaptive, communicative, academic, or other personal social skills.

As we move forward through this book, I hope that we will become comfortable with each other so that you, the reader, will become you, the doer, and you, the support system, for the mentally retarded: in this way, we will improve the world in which these individuals live and function.

The semantic content or division of mental retardation into functional or adaptive behavior levels is not meant to be a process of stereotyping. It was felt to be of value to differentiate various approaches used with groups of individuals sharing similar learning styles and adaptive behaviors. Thus, classifications are used in a functional, pragmatic way. These generalizations reflect the feelings and perceptions of the author and her experiences in the real "clinical world" of sex education and sex counseling. The case histories reflect experiences of the author and her co-professionals throughout the nation. Names used are fictitious.

This material is presented as a sharing of ideas, feelings, and experiences in hopes that it will allow others to use it as a sounding board to explore their own creativity and to pursue specific areas of interest in as much depth as will be meaningful to any specific reader. The theories and principles of this book are applicable and easily adaptable to other special populations. This clinical and therapeutic guidebook should aid adults in helping all special people develop healthy psychosocial-sexual attitudes and personalities. This is proposed as a catalytic beginning.

ACKNOWLEDGEMENTS

In appreciation to my chidren, David and Adam, and my parents, Irma and Isadore Kramer, who showed me patience and understanding for the time taken from them while developing this project.

To Dr. Erbert F. Cicenia, the entire staff of the South Carolina Department of Mental Retardation, both in the Central Office and the Coastal Region, especially Jim Hill, General Counsel, and Jim Taylor, Director of Planning and Grants, for their advice, and to the residents of the South Carolina Department of Mental Retardation for helping me to grow and to experience. To the American Association of Sex Educators, Counselors, and Therapists for its impact on my development, especially Winifred Kempton, who has been my mentor.

To Dr. James Semens, Dr. Paul Fleming, Mary Anne Fisher, Dr. Oliver Bjorkson, Dr. and Mrs. J. Chambers, Dr. Sandra Catoe, and Richard Henderson, all of whom have lent their support. Also, for their technical help, I would like to thank Charlotte Bright, Terrie Mylin, Juli Boyer, JoAnn Spangler, Irma Kramer, Judy Wolper, Dr. Conrad Kottak, Dr. Albert Warshauer, Bill Langley, Dr. George Leighton, Dr. Ron Kirschner, and Dr. James McLean. To each and every one, I owe a debt of gratitude for patience and encouragement.

I am personally and professionally indebted to Marianna Roberts, M.S.W., ACSW, RSW, for her devotion and support, and for the time given to review this work in detail. Mrs. Roberts offered in-depth consultation concerning her analysis of the clinical and therapeutic value of this book, and its application to the practicing clinician.

A note of special appreciation is also extended to George Moskowitz, M.D., FABFP; and Jackson S. Howell, Jr., Ph.D., Clinical Psychologist, for their review and comments on the manuscript.

Special thanks to Thomas Shipp, Ph.D., who first suggested that I share this information in writing and introduced me to College-Hill Press. Dr Shipp also provided me with some valuable initial editorial help and advice.

chapter one

SEXUALITY

Sexuality: Maleness, femaleness, sensuality, sense of self, ego, perception of self in relationship to the world and others, the quality or state of being sexual — the condition of having sexual activity or intercourse, expression or receiving and expressing sexual interest... Any of these terms or all of them easily could be a definition of sexuality. For most people, sexuality connotes a very personal definition and produces specific meanings and thought processes derived from experiences that have happened from birth to whatever stage of development they have reached at the present time.

Sexuality is expressed through sensuality. The mentally retarded can effectively use the various senses to explore and enjoy themselves and their worlds in ways acceptable to their living environments and society. The mentally retarded will do this respective to their adaptive levels of functioning.

Sexuality is an evolving instinctive type of behavior. Responses are not related to the level of mental retardation. The expression of sexuality is inhibited, restricted, and defined by societal rules that do not readily recognize the mentally retarded population as having positive, responsible sexual development.

In the normal population, it is well accepted that people are sexual and have sexuality that they may choose to express or not express within certain societal constraints. For the purposes of this book, emphasis will not be placed on this normal population.

Interpretation and relationships to the field of sexuality within the population considered to be not normal, will be referred to as the mentally retarded. As mentioned in the introduction, this is not for the purpose of stereotyping, but to establish some definitive guidelines that will allow the reader to know the *basic perspective* from which the author is writing and perceiving the behaviors being discussed. The American Association of Mental Deficiency uses the categories of mild, moderate, severe, and profound retardation with associated intelligence quotients. For the purpose of this book, the general areas will be used in a clinical sense; however, the specific IQ scores will not be employed, as it is not felt that the process would increase meaning or comprehension of the subject matter.

The American Association of Mental Deficiency broadly interprets mental retardation as significant subaverage intelligence of more than two standard deviations below the mean of 100, with problems in adaptive functioning that occur prior to the age of eighteen, i.e., during the developmental period. The impairment in adaptive functioning is the area that will most directly affect the development of sexuality and expression of sexuality with the mentally retarded population.

In understanding the dynamics of mental retardation, it helps to examine the behaviors exhibited by the different subgroups of mental retardation. Just as all nonretarded individuals are approached in ways which meet their specific needs, the same can be done with the mentally retarded. All concerned need to have the same *point of reference* in understanding the characteristics of the groups being discussed.

The family unit recognizes at some point of maturation in early infancy or childhood that the adaptive behavior of the individual is, in fact, maladaptive and noncompliant to societal and familial expectations. This results in an assessment of behavior in relationship to standard examination tools and current understanding. At this point, help is sought to identify and remediate the problems. Professionals until this time, unfortunately, have focused mainly on maladaptive behavior as it relates to ability to perform in school or other learning situations.

A broader level of human interaction must be considered, i.e., sexual behavior as it is expressed. The mild, moderate, severe, and profound levels of mental retardation will be explored in terms of sexuality. These groupings will be used as *reference points* to study the element of sexuality. The mentally retarded will be considered as sexual human beings, with various levels of development, adaptive behavior, and coping skills. Exploring the adaptive behavior of the mentally retarded and searching for solutions and programs will help foster the development of appropriate and acceptable interactions in a psychosocial-sexual way within the family, society, and the community-at-large.

In developing a program to foster healthy psychosocial-sexual development, there is an urgent need to recognize the social aspects of development on a personal, private level, as well as a public, community, and familial level. Professional and societal biases increase the handicap by isolating the sexual composition of the individual labeled mentally retarded.

Following are some outlined suggested common points of the subgroups of mental retardation and behavioral characteristics that might be helpful in understanding these groups and their general coping abilities. These generally accepted levels suggest certain behavioral characteristics that might be meaningful in understanding the subgroups. As such, they can be used as *reference points* for the reader.

Mildly Mentally Retarded
— Similar to average or normative psychosocial-sexual behavior in society
— Explores, adapts, controls sexual impulses and urges in similar ways as majority of society
— Responds to verbal modes of sex education/sex counseling/sex therapy
— Capable of developing appropriate adaptive skills with current sex education/sex counseling/sex therapy methods

Moderately Mentally Retarded
— Secondary sexual characteristics might be delayed
— Adaptive and psychosocial-sexual behavior not readily accessible to individual
— Functions more on a primary reward and primitive reinforcement system level
— May respond to verbal mode of sex education/sex counseling to develop more appropriate adaptive behavior; however, may require techniques of behavior modification systems to be effective

Severely Mentally Retarded
— Very poor control of sexual impulses
— Lack of development of adaptive psychosocial-sexual behavior
— Limited ability to predict or to foresee consequences of sensual/sexual behavior
— Problems comprehending societal rules, especially *private* versus *public*, and developing adaptive behavior in these areas

— The technique of behavior modification may be most effective in creating change in this group.

Profoundly Mentally Retarded
— Function primarily by having basic needs met
— Very little adaptive behavior
— Predominant reactions are impulsive
— Limited ability to predict or foresee consequences of sensual/sexual behavior
— Minimal recognizable adaptive skills
— Pleasure seeking frequently in self-stimulating way
— Often masturbates excessively or in harmful way
— Techniques of behavior modification must be used to affect change

Understanding these different levels of retardation will help the reader gain a better perspective of the positive and negative complications inherent in providing sexual training and counseling to the mentally retarded. Consideration of the individual personality qualities of each retarded person is important. This ensures the type of service which is their right.

The final goal to be explored is the sexuality of the mentally retarded individual within socially approved environments for the release of the expression of sexuality. This will better ensure a similar treatment of sexuality in the mentally retarded, as in the normal population. Clinical and therapeutic approaches will be used for understanding and coping with this process.

chapter two

SEXUALITY AND RELATIONSHIP TO LEVELS OF RETARDATION

Different ways of subdividing the levels of mental retardation were explored. The simplest and most direct way was a division into categories of mild, moderate, severe, and profound mental retardation. Each person is indeed an individual. There are always dangers inherent in generalizing to specific categories. However, this process does allow a common base of understanding.

It should be clearly understood that whenever subcategories are used, generalizations are employed. Thus, these subgroups are only used as a suggested division or as a way of approaching the mentally retarded population in a more specific way. All competent clinical and therapeutic interaction must keep the individualism of the client foremost in mind.

Different problems are encountered with emerging sexuality at the different levels of mental retardation. The four categories of mild, moderate, severe and profound mental retardation will be explored with respect to sexual problems encountered, examples of the ways the problems are exhibited, and possible solutions to these problems.

SEXUALITY AND THE MILDLY MENTALLY RETARDED

On the whole, the mildly mentally retarded population can be treated much like the population of nonretarded people. The mildly mentally retarded will have various abilities and skills in recognizing and meeting their sexual needs. There are many mildly mentally retarded individuals who live their lives within society, never having been identified as mentally retarded. They might be the individuals who appear at family planning clinics and who are unable to read or understand informed consent forms, when presented to them.

The mildly retarded often lack the adaptive skills to know how to take care of their personal and psychosocial-sexual needs by using community resources. Once these individuals are shown how to use the resources and are given a system that works for them, they function most effectively. With this population, the goal of the sex educator/sex counselor is to help integrate these individuals, as much as possible, into the mainstream of society — helping them adjust to their handicaps and limitations. They need to be taught how to use community resources to the best of their ability.

The mildly retarded can be naive about birth control, venereal disease, sexual intercourse, masturbation, parenting, and marriage. However, they do desire to have psychosocial-sexual relationships and often enter into sexual encounters easily, without anticipating the long range consequences. This population can receive ongoing sex education and sex counseling when needed to help them make the best adjustment to society that they can make. Education should not begin at age twenty but rather at birth, as done with any nonretarded child.

One of the major problems possible to encounter with the mildly retarded is that they have sexual urges and desires but have not learned the social amenities that will allow them to meet these needs without being abusive to themselves or others. The retarded function on a very concrete language level. It is often difficult for them to acquire the subtleties of sexuality that the nonretarded learn through observation.

The mildly retarded are apt to react instinctively more than rationally. If the mentally retarded become involved in a sexual encounter that feels good, they are not likely to stop to analyze the appropriateness of the act and then decide whether to act or not. These are skills that can and should be taught. It is in this way that the mildly retarded will develop better adaptive skills and lead more enriching sexual lives.

Example A:
A mildly mentally retarded female who was three months pregnant appeared at an abortion clinic. The abortion counselor found on the intake interview that she was retarded

and did not have any knowledge of what caused her pregnancy — only that there was a baby inside of her. Assessment also showed that there was no knowledge of birth control or interest in using birth control after the desired abortion. The abortion counselor was leery of the situation because she did not feel that the retarded woman was able to understand the informed consent form. The abortion counselor handled the situation by providing some basic sex education which involved drawings and discussions of anatomy, physiology, conception, contraception, pregnancy, etc.

The retarded woman was then sent home to think about the information and consider use of birth control after the abortion. A few days later, the retarded woman returned to the abortion clinic to see the counselor again. The counselor was able to ascertain that the woman understood the information provided on the previous visit. The woman now freely admitted that she had had sexual intercourse with a man, which was how she became pregnant. She also verbalized a willingness to use birth control (in this case an IUD) after the abortion. At this point the abortion counselor said that she felt comfortable enough with the woman's knowledge to allow her to make her *mark* on the informed consent form and proceeded with the abortion arrangements.

This example shows appropriate caution and good counseling skills on the part of the abortion counselor. Responsibility was assumed for helping the mildly retarded woman become more responsible for herself sexually. A certified sex educator/sex counselor involved with community agencies can apprise them of the limitations and needs of the mildly retarded population.

Example B:
A mildly mentally retarded adult female living at home with her mother and stepfather has been masturbating and enjoying it for years. The stepfather approaches her, begins fondling her breasts and entices her to have sexual intercourse, but threatens to punish her if she tells her mother. The young woman enjoys sex with the stepfather but feels that there must be something wrong with this behavior or he would not have warned her not to tell her mother. The incidents continue frequently.

Later the woman attends a residential program and is sexually active. When counseled about her sexual activity, she relates experiences about her stepfather and what they used to do. The mother is called and the stepfather is confronted. He does not deny the incidents but the mother refuses to bring legal charges. The most that the residential program can do is take the matter to court and make the recommendation that the retarded woman not be allowed to visit the home as long as the stepfather is there. The retarded woman is then counseled about appropriate sex partners and incest. This was not a case of rape as the retarded woman was an eager and willing partner but the stepfather certainly was not an appropriate partner for her to choose or cooperate with sexually.

The frequency of incest with the mildly retarded may be quite high. The mildly mentally retarded, who may tend to react basically on the pleasure principle, can easily be led and coerced into behavior that otherwise might be considered abusive or inappropriate.

The mildly mentally retarded are often viewed as having very poor self imagery and self worth. Consequently, they sometimes sell themselves short or cheap, literally, with respect to sexuality. It is not uncommon in a residential facility to find the bartering system in effect of "I'll buy you a coke if you'll go behind the bushes and f--- with me." Since sexual intercourse usually is seen as a pleasurable activity, the female will often cooperate and not "tell" for the price of a coke. The sex educator/sex counselor's task is to improve self concept and self worth, emphasize that friendship and sex not be bought, and that saying "no" is a very acceptable answer.

Example C:
A young moderately retarded adult female was living in a residential facility. She was very sexually active with a variety of partners. When counseled about her sexual activity, it surfaced that she only enjoyed sex with one of these partners. However, because the other men would always buy her an extra coke, she would let them take her in the woods or behind a building and have sex. The young woman had to be taught to say "no" when she did not want to have sex, to separate her sexual feeling from her desire for sodas, and to be given a way to earn money so that she could buy the cokes without having to barter for sex to procure them.

The goal of the sex counseling was not to extinguish her sexual behavior, but to make it more meaningful and more appropriate. This was accomplished as she began to refuse the partners she did not like and had a way to earn money to buy treats. She also began to focus more of her attention on the man that she did like. Thus, she began to develop a more meaningful relationship within which to explore her sexuality.

Before moving to a less restrictive environment, especially a living situation in the community, these were valuable skills for her to learn so that she would not be easy prey to pimps, prostitutes, or others who would take advantage of her. The sex counseling was accomplished through individual counseling sessions where role playing, cognitive restructuring, and alternate solutions were sought during the counseling intervention process.

Optimal survival in the *real world — community-at-large* is very difficult for someone with lowered educational, cognitive, and adaptive skills. Advantage can be taken of these mentally retarded people by negative and abusive forces because of their limited experiences and reasoning skills.

For the mildly retarded, who have the ability to comprehend and act on it, one of the most important concepts to teach is that "your body is a private part of you. You are responsible for your own body and no one else can touch or hurt your body without force, unless you want them to or allow them to touch you. If someone wants to touch you or do something that you do not want, say "No," yell for help, get help, or fight. Learning not to be compliant is very important in helping the mildly retarded adjust to community living and nonretarded peer pressure.

Example D:

A young mildly retarded adult male had a medical condition that made him look quite different from his peers. He felt very self-conscious and had a very poor self-concept. As he passed through puberty and began developing sexual feelings, he experimented extensively with masturbation. He then wanted to participate in mutual masturbation. His past experiences at dances and other social events was that females would not pay attention to him, even if he "got up his nerve" and asked them to dance.

He began to look at the male population for a willing partner. Here he also found difficulty unless he bought his way with gifts or food items. He became quite successful at getting other males to cooperate with him in the passive role during anal intercourse, which he enjoyed. He did not consider himself *homosexual* and was offended when someone called him "gay or queer," but he was making no movement to develop his own sexuality in a heterosexual way.

He very much wanted to be community-bound. At this time, he entered sex counseling. Goals of sex counseling were to increase self-esteem, ego, and body imagery, give information, and make sure that he had awareness of the positives and negatives of being involved in the homosexual community-at-large. He was apprised of what special risks he might be taking because of his handicap and vulnerability due to his looking different. The sex counselor helped this man accept himself and look for an alternate solution to expressing his sexual feelings. In this case, masturbation was encouraged and the use of *girlie* magazines with erotic pictures was suggested to help him develop a fantasy level. *Privacy* was also stressed, as was careful choosing of partners from those he knew (without purchasing their favors).

He was encouraged to explore his ability to be more social and develop more ability to have fun with females on a nonsexual basis so that eventually a friendship might lead to an affectionate and possible heterosexual experience. By using a coeducational sex counseling group, that did a great deal of affirming this man, his imagery of self and behavior began to become more acceptable and appropriate to his environment. He was eventually told that he could make a choice about coming to the sex counseling sessions since he had achieved all of his goals. Surprisingly, he chose to continue to come. The coeducational counseling sessions had become a positive socialization experience for him.

A successful sex counseling group for the mentally retarded will do just that: become a vehicle for developing pleasant and positive fun oriented, nonsexual encounters. It is also an open forum where men and women are able to talk freely about their feelings about self, each other, their expectations, and how they can help each other achieve these or modify behavior when it is needed. There is no better pressure than peer pressure. The sex counselor leading these types of sessions is only a facilitator and giver of information. Role playing and re-enacting the experiences that have been negative help turn them into positive feelings and productive learning experiences.

Historically, parents and professionals, on the whole, underestimate the abilities of the mentally retarded to enter into and profit from this type of counseling session. This helping system can be explored more frequently to see if it has somethng to offer the individual — especially in the mildly retarded range of functioning ability. Community mental health centers can incorporate such a program and have it available for handicapped and mentally retarded individuals living in the community. The reality, however, is that in most communities, if a person is not living in a residential center where there is qualified staff to help with sexual problems, there might be difficulty finding the service in the community due to a lack of resources.

Example E:

A mildly retarded adult in her mid-forties (who had given birth to a child early in life) was living in a residential center. Periodically she went through cycles of being very sexually active, choosing any willing partner. When her sexual behavior became blatantly obvious, the staff referred her to the sex counselor. During the sex counseling sessions many traditional things were discussed but one question that the woman asked remained vivid in the counselor's memory. The woman said, "What is it supposed to feel like?" When asked if she was referring to sexual intercourse, the woman indicated "yes." Here was a woman, who had given birth many years before, had lived in several different facilities, and had had a multitude of sexual partners. She was quite verbal, had good reading skills; yet in total honesty and innocence she wanted her question answered. It appeared that she had never had an orgasm, but was just enjoying the male attention and closeness of the male body. On some level, she knew that there should have been more.

Is this situation so different from many of the nonretarded population who have not been helped to feel good about their sexuality and the feelings that they could have with sexual activity? This woman was encouraged to masturbate to see if she could achieve some positive feelings from clitoral stimulation. She was also encouraged to stop being promiscuous.

Follow-up counseling sessions showed that she was beginning to have some positive sexual feelings in her clitoral area, she was more aware of the orgasmic response, and that she was being more discriminating about her overt sexual activity. In essence, she had developed more inner control over her sexual feelings and responses. During the sessions, she was never told that she was *bad to act out sexually* but, rather, that she was choosing inappropriate partners in an environment that had rules against sexual intercourse. Therefore, she was calling attention to herself and giving staff no option but to report her behavior when she exhibited it so publicly.

With the mildly mentally retarded males and females, it can easily be seen that they have the potential for developing good positive feelings about their sexuality regardless of handicap. It takes the support, information-giving and permission-giving, along with a supporting, nonjudgmental environment in which they can grow.

MILDLY RETARDED WITH PHYSICAL HANDICAPS

One population not addressed above are the mildly mentally retarded who also have some degree of physical handicap such as cerebral palsy, ranging from mild to severe. The sex education/sex counseling goals are the same for this group as for the nonphysically involved. Sexual fulfillment is harder for them to achieve and harder, too, for parents, professionals,and communities to acknowledge and accept. All of the options mentioned in this book can be made available to this population. Special situations can be established where they too will be able to participate in sex education/sex counseling sessions with qualified people with whom they are comfortable. They can process their frustrations concerning their sexuality and the limitations placed upon them by their bodies and learn to function regardless.

The movie "Like Other People" is excellent. It was made in England and shows a society that has supported and understood the needs of physically handicapped couples who choose to live together without marriage. Public acceptance in America does not seem to be at this point yet. It should be noted that certain communities and states are making great strides in this area.

Example F:

A group of male and female young cerebral palsy adults were living together in a cottage in a residential facility for the mentally retarded. Were they truly retarded? This is a difficult question to answer because testing techniques for this population are so poor. However, the social skills of this group were quite high. The group members appeared to be mildly retarded. Sexual feelings and urges were developing rapidly; and yet, no one had consistently worked with the members of this group (eight females and fifteen males) to explain much about sex education, why they were going through body changes, feelings, etc. One female who had had a hysterectomy was never told she was sterile. Although she was completely and irreversibly quadraplegic and nonverbal, she had expectations and fantasies that one day she would have a child.

The nurse in charge and the sex educator decided that it was time to do some aggressive and very open sex education with the group. The cottage parents were gathered for a preliminary discussion, along with all natural parents who desired to attend. It was decided to have the nurse and sex educator take the females and males separately and then work with them together in a coeducational setting.

The goal was to give information, develop feelings, appropriate coping techniques, and then help the group develop acceptable easy ways to deal with some of the frustrations that they were encountering. Their living environment was very restrictive with respect to their exhibiting any sexuality or developing any permanent love relationship due to their physical limitations. Helping people accept the environmental living limitations that currently cannot be changed is one of the goals of a sex education/sex counseling program.

The group was multihandicapped and the skill level of the group leaders was very important, because augmentative/alternative modes of communication had to be used. In addition, some very skillful role playing was required where the group leaders had to serve as catalysts and perform much of what the physically handicapped were not able to do. This technique was accomplished using the many support personnel that normally interacted with the group, including psychologists, nurses, recreators, and cottage parents.

The culmination of the sessions was that the coeducational group decided to plan a holiday party where they would have the opportunity to demonstrate some of the new appropriate socialization behavior they had been taught. They all assumed responsibilities for preparing the party, entertainment, and invitation list. It was very successful, with wheelchair dancing and live music. The party helped prove the point that being in a wheelchair did not have to be antithetical to having a good time. These types of positive socialization experiences are far too scarce for this physically handicapped population that also has some degree of mental retardation. All efforts should be made to open more doors and avenues for these individuals in all environments.

THE PHYSICALLY HANDICAPPED PERSON WITH NORMAL INTELLIGENCE

It should be noted for those who are interested in studying further, that a very different set of circumstances exists for those people who have normal intelligence but are physically handicapped either from birth defect, accident, or war injury. Society seems to accept readily that these people, especially those who have been injured as adults, are sexual human beings, most of whom led active sexual lives before receiving injury. Therefore, it is not unusual to expect them to be sexual afterwards.

It is thus very acceptable for the medical, psychological, and family support systems to work with these physically handicapped and the partners of their choice, whether in or out of marriage, to help them lead active sexual lives again. No one hesitates to use sexual aids or prostheses with this group, nor questions their rights to be sexual. It is not difficult for this population to find support and helping systems to aid them in their fight to achieve sexual independence and fulfillment. Why can this not also become a reality for the physically handicapped who are mildly retarded? The hope is that this will become an actuality in the future. Some of the bibliography and related interest references show that this process has begun.

SEXUALITY AND THE MODERATELY MENTALLY RETARDED

With the moderately mentally retarded, the emergence of a special problem arises: For the most part, this population does not easily assimilate into society nor share many of the resources that make the mildly retarded look so similar to the mainstream of society. Because of their lowered adaptive, cognitive, and educational skills, this group can be identified more easily by the public as mentally retarded. The behavior of the moderately mentally retarded becomes suspect to those unfamiliar with it. Reading, coping, and judgment skills are usually low, and this group is often academically trainable instead of being educable.

Does this mean that they are any different sexually? No, they are not, but their ability to handle their sexuality and privileges and consequences of their sexual behavior must be taught to them in a more pragmatic and programmed way. This is the level at which good programmers will begin using effective behavior modification techniques. Environments will have to be more structured and protective so that these people can grow and develop to the best of their abilities and skills.

Sexual behavior, self-stimulation, and nondiscriminative mutual masturbation, often ending in same or opposite sex intercourse, can be exhibited. This behavior is very difficult for parents, professionals, and caregivers to accept. For the mildly mentally retarded, a good case can be made for allowing them to be sexual because they can be taught to be responsible sexually. However, the question asked about the moderately retarded is whether they can be taught to be responsible sexually. Yes, they can but it may be at a different level. Sexual expresson may not involve traditional relationships as much as self-experimentation. Sex education should emphasize (1) the discovery of masturbation, (2) teaching appropriate masturbation, (3) how not to take advantage of others or let oneself get abused, and (4) how to behave appropriately in *public* so that it will not be cause for trouble with community standards or with the law regarding such things as *indecent exposure.*

Example G:
A moderately mentally retarded male was taken on a field trip into the community. He was walking through an open park. He felt the need to urinate but did not see an enclosed bathroom (even though programmers had taught him to sight read the bathroom words *boy and men,* this did him no good as there were no bathrooms in sight). Because his bladder was full and he had a need to relieve himself, he went to the nearest bush. He disregarded the fact that there were children and adults around him, unzipped his pants, took out his penis, and commenced to urinate. At that time, a parent in the park was highly disturbed and found a policeman who came to arrest the man because of *indecent exposure.* The man was taken to jail where it was ascertained that he was retarded and the charges

were dropped.

In this case, the parents and programmers of this man were amiss to send him into the community alone without first teaching him the difference between appropriate and inappropriate responses to having to urinate when there was not a visible bathroom.

Example H:

A moderately retarded male was in jail. The charge was *child molestation*. He had been living at home with several young nieces and nephews who liked to play with him because he would squat on the floor and play harmlessly at their level, which many adults would not do. He had never been warned about not playing with strangers' children.

He was daily being programmed at a work activity center and was acting as a helper to an electrician. The electrician took him on a service call. The family had a six-year-old daughter. While the electrician was fixing the washing machine, the retarded man disappeared for a few minutes but the electrician, busy in his work, did not pay attention to it. All of a sudden, the electrician heard the mother of the child yelling hysterically, "Leave my daughter alone." The electrician went to find out what had happened. The little girl, awed by the retarded man's interest in talking to her, had invited him into her bedroom to play with her dolls. The mother found them sitting on the floor playing. The little girl happened to be sitting in the lap of the retarded man, and the mother wanted to press charges for *child molestation.*

Sounds ridiculous? Maybe. However, it is true and not uncommon. What is the answer? The moderately retarded male who may not be capable of making the judgment independently that he should not play in strange bedrooms with little girls must specifically be taught and conditioned that this behavior is unacceptable and, as such, will get him into trouble with the law. He must understand that he just cannot do it. He should be made aware of the consequences of his behavior. Again a competent lawyer intervened but the damage to all parties was unnecessary in the first place, and should and could have been avoided. How many people are incarcerated that should not be for such similar incidents?

The moderately retarded often have good verbal skills and can be very manipulative with them. They are often told they can not do something because they are retarded or stupid, or both. This lingo becomes part of their language experience and coping system.

It is not unusual to have either a moderately retarded male or female say to a counselor, "I can't do that because I'm retarded." When this happens, the person needs to be confronted with exactly what his handicap entails and what it means with regard to being able to function as other human beings. These individuals should not be allowed to "cop out" on terms that they do not even understand, e.g., "I'm retarded." The moderately retarded, too, can be taught that they are responsible for their bodies and actions. It will just take longer and may require more behavior modification techniques than with the normal or mildly retarded.

Reinforcement charts and rewards that are tangible and frequent are very reinforcing to this group. Reinforcement or punishment should not be delayed. Contingencies must be appropriate and immediate so that they will be effective. Parents and educators alike can be encouraged by the sex educator/sex counselor to have high expectations that this moderately retarded group can function as responsible sexual adults.

Masturbation is to be encouraged specifically with this group. Some moderately retarded individuals will have the capacity to develop caring and loving relationships that involve sex. Others will develop sporadic sexual relationships but all can learn to pleasure themselves, both females and males.

Tremendous emphasis usually is placed on the male learning how to masturbate. The same amount of time and effort should be spent teaching and educating the female how to masturbate to climax also. The female should be instructed about breast and clitoral stimulation and told of the ways in which she can stimulate herself in a nonharmful way. This factor is most important so that she will not use harmful objects in the masturbatory process.

Example I:
An adult moderately retarded female was found using a coke bottle to masturbate. She was asked to remove the coke bottle. She was told that this bottle could break and cut her vagina, causing her pain and requiring her to see the doctor. She was encouraged to use her hand (especially while bathng, because the soap would provide some lubrication and keep her from

rubbing herself rough or dry), a soft toy, or object, but not to use coke bottles.

If the caregiver, instead, had just said, "You are doing something bad. Stop it," and had not given the woman alternate solutions on how to stimulate herself, negative feelings about masturbation might have developed. The use of harmful objects might have continued.

It is time for adults to realize and deal with the fact that the sexuality and sexual urges of the moderately retarded will not just go away or disappear bceause the adult wants them to do so. If that is the approach, or if things such as the above incident are ignored, the results will be failure of any attempted programming.

The moderately retarded males and females often use a great deal of street language because it seems that is all they hear with reference to sexual terminology. People have questioned whether these individuals can learn words such as vagina, breasts, intercourse, masturbation — because they are hard words to say and remember. Certainly, it is true that the moderately retarded may not learn these words as easily as higher level invididuals. However, all efforts should be made from birth to use the proper terminology for body parts with this population. This will increase the probability of receptively and expressively teaching this vocabulary. Without exposure to the specific words, they will never be learned nor their terminology understood. However, the expressed behavior will still exist. Hence, why not try to deal with it openly and directly. The moderately retarded are also a population that need to be taught techniques of self-control to substitute for their often poor impulse control.

Many Down's Syndrome adults are often perceived by the general population as very affectionate and loving human beings. Because families and professionals find this to be a positive trait and not disruptive, very little attention is often paid to teaching this group of individuals how to behave socially in a manner appropriate for their age, e.g., greeting people by handshakes instead of hugs. It should be every adult's responsibility to encourage appropriate greetings regardless of the level of mental retardation. The moderately retarded person who is constantly hugging and kissing strangers is bound to eventually end in a situation which is, at least, compromising and one which cannot be easily handled.

Dancing can be a very enjoyable outlet for most people. The moderately retarded can easily use this as a good and positive social activity. First, individuals need to learn the skills of dancing. This would also apply to wheelchair-bound people who can participate in wheelchair dancing. Actual programs need to be organized which role play asking a person to dance, accepting the invitation, proper behavior on the dance floor, and the appropriate way to hold some one without being overtly sexual. These are skills that usually are not learned instinctively by many of the retarded population. However, they are skills that can be effectively taught. It is the responsibility of the programmer to teach these skills. Again, operant conditioning, using shaping techniques, and reinforcement systems, such as real dances, dressy clothes, and live bands can help make this a viable option for teaching these behavior skills to the moderately retarded.

Most moderately retarded people will have to live in some sort of protected or restricted environment. That does not mean that their lives have to be void of pleasurable and pleasuring experiences in a psychosocial-sexual way. All efforts should be made to encourage the development of appropriate socialization skills including dating and courting skills for those capable of handling these situations. The job of the professional is to assess what information is necessary for that particular individual to learn to live an enriched life and what techniques are necessary to help teach these skills. All of this can fit into the protective and restricted environment, making it a more acceptable and normal-type living environment for this population of moderately retarded individuals. Thus, this will allow them the privilege of leading much fuller and richer lives, and of expressing their sexuality within their capabilities and the limitations of the environment.

SEXUALITY AND THE SEVERELY MENTALLY RETARDED

The severely mentally retarded population can include many different types of multihandicaps. Usually family and programs are intensely involved in multi-remedial programs which try to enhance environmental awareness and self-awareness so that their quality of life and general well-being are sustained and improved, if possible. It is not unusual, under these circumstances, to think of sexuality last when thinking of need fulfillment. In this population, as with the profoundly retarded, primary needs often involve medical-therapeutic techniques; including proper positioning, feeding, range of motion exercises, establishing any basic signal communication, consciousness of self, and awareness of environment.

In Chapter 9, the reader can explore in-depth about self-stimulation and the mentally retarded. Excessive self-stimulatory activities are often exhibited by both the severely and profoundly retarded groups. The programmer has to assess the difference in perseverative self-stimulation, whether genitally directed or not. A need may exist to develop operant conditioning programs to control the problem, if it is becoming harmful to the individual. Although it sounds oversimplified to say that all behavior can be shaped by operant conditioning, a skilled programmer can take advantage of the techniques of operant conditioning and pair that with intensive work by the staff, achieving consistency and getting positive results from almost any potentially negative situation.

Example J:

The director of psychology in a residential facility called the sex counselor for assistance in developing a program for an adolescent severely retarded autistic male who had begun taking his penis and putting it in the mouth of any other child he could find, male or female. The staff was most upset and wanted an immediate solution. A solution was offered, which was effective within thirty-six hours, the length of time necessary to extinguish the undesired behavior. Sign language and total communication, which means that the caregiver talks while signing, were being used in the living environment. Staff were instructed to do the following: Every time that the retarded person took his penis and attempted to have fellatio with another resident, the staff person was to approach the situation, say and sign "Stop, penis in pants." Simultaneously the male was gently led by the arm into a toilet stall where he could be alone to do whatever he chose.

This redirection was done to show him that the toilet area was an acceptable private place to have his penis out of his pants. When the individual came out of the toilet stall, the staff person was instructed to say, while signing "Penis in pants, zip your pants," and then lead the person back to the group. Everytime the behavior was exhibited, the staff was to follow with the above actions. Keeping the communication simple and restricted to the above phrases, all presented in a total communication mode, and having the staff members always use the same reaction of removing the male from the situation and into the bathroom, helped extinguish the oral sex behavior.

The success of this simple technique within the short time period of thirty- six hours is indicative of how easy it can be to extinguish behavior or to condition incompatible responses, if the staff is well trained in these techniques. Therefore, it is well worth the administrative time to teach these techniques to the staff as extensively as possible, until they are comfortable and competent in the skills. This time spent will ensure improvement in all areas of programming.

Example K:
A deaf/blind severely retarded adult male seemed to have no awareness of anyone around him or of his environment in general. He would masturbate for hours on end, regardless of the program, and regardless of whether he was clothed in overalls that he could not unzip or in pajamas that he could remove while in bed. He would masturbate in bed to the extent that the bed would shake and make lots of noise.

The other deaf/blind residents were not affected by this behavior, but the staff was upset and wanted the behavior to stop. Most staff members were open and honest enough to say that they thought the problem was that the male was never climaxing and therefore was always sexually frustrated. To some extent, that might have been the case. However, in all probability, the masturbation had just become a perseverative self-stimulating behavior because no other efforts to bring external stimuli into this man's personal world were working. The sex counselor worked with the staff, letting them know that the act of masturbation was all right. In this case, however, when it went on for hours at a time, it was felt that masturbation was becoming nonpurposeful. Because of the environment , no "hands on" techniques of teaching and/or assisting in the masturbatory process were allowed. The only solutions available were to look intensively at available programming that would condition an incompatible response, such as having the man do something with both of his hands that was perseverative but nonmastubatory. This was a very difficult case. It finally had to be accepted that there was little that the staff could do regarding the excessive masturbation in the bed, during sleeping hours. A very direct and forceful stand was taken during programming hours to try and condition incompatible responses to the excessive masturbation.

The staff was minimally successful in getting the individual involved in behaviors that were incompatible with masturbation. Total success was never achieved with this case as far as the ideal, e.g., reducing the excessive masturbation to a point where it was purposefully directed toward a climax. The individual could proceed to another activity. The staff could never invade the self-stimulating world to the necessary extent. They had to accept the slight bit of improvement they could get and to readjust their thinking, realizing that it was not harmful and negative for the masturbation to be excessive at times.

The staff or parents of a severely retarded individual, whether male or female, have trouble accepting that there is emerging sexuality and sexual feelings within this group. Therefore, while providing daily care, such as bathing, the caregiver is often surprised and disturbed by erections of the males and/or excessive movements of the females while the genitals are being stimulated. For the physically multihandicapped who are not able to move their arms enough to get them to their genital areas, this bathing stimulation of the genitals may be the only time they have pleasurable sexual type feelings. In the case of males, staff should not be upset if ejaculate appears during the bathing process. They should just treat it calmly as a normal situation, cleaning the genital area, and continuing with the bathing. The same would be true of caregiving in the middle of the night and dealing with erections and ejaculate in the bedroom situation. With females, the caregiver should be aware that bathing of the breasts and genital area will be stimulating and can cause a sexual response. This is to be expected. Such behavior is all right and should be handled calmly and pragmatically.

If the caregiver feels comfortable with discussing the behavior with the mentally retarded person, very simple language should be used to explain what body parts are being washed. Communication should state that it is known that it feels good to be touched and that it is part of getting a bath or being taken care of when you can not take care of yourself. More than likely, the erection, ejaculation, or female sexual response can most comfortably be handled by the caregiver just completing the job in a calm and systematic manner.

The ambulatory severely retarded often will try to explore the bodies of other severely retarded individuals with whom they live. Caregivers have to be careful to protect the rights of privacy of everyone involved in the living environment. Again, simple direct language or communication systems should be used, in addition to removal from the situation when not appropriate.

Under no circumstances would it seem acceptable for the severely retarded to be allowed to explore the bodies of nonretarded children or adults who are unwilling to participate. Any efforts in this direction should be extinguished by the caregivers. Contingencies should be set to make this programming more effective. The seeking of affection should be recognized and reciprocated in an appropriate nonsexual way, so that the severely retarded will not feel rejection.

The caregivers and other significant people in the environment need to be careful not to send signals that are sexual in nature, rather than just being nurturing and affectionate. This returns to the concept of the infantalization of the mentally retarded. Everyone must realize that the baby or young child grows to become an adult with adult feelings, urges, and sexuality, regardless of the level of mental retardation. It is, therefore, the responsibility of the adults and caregivers to respond appropriately, teaching appropriate responses whenever possible.

One of the main problems encountered with the severely retarded population is in the area of masturbation. It is very difficult to get this population to realize that masturbation is an act to do in *private, not public*. This is covered in great detail in Chapter 9, so will just be mentioned here. In order for the severely retarded to be able to enjoy the benefits of socializing with other people, whether retarded or not, they need to develop enough appropriate social behavior so that they will be welcome within the group. If the severely retarded are constantly digging at their genitals in *public*, the tendency of the caregivers will be to keep them from being in *public* because it embarrasses the caregiver. It is very beneficial to the severely retarded to receive enough help in this area to help them learn to discriminate and control sexual behavior in *public*. Also, it will give them more access to others and more opportunities to participate in the activities that are available to them, on the whole.

Appropriate social behavior, sexual or not, should be taught, conditioned whenever possible, and always reinforced appropriately so that the likelihood of its increasing and being used will be more probable. This will also help in emptying the back wards of the institutions and will bring those individuals previously closeted in homes more into the mainstream of life. In general, this will improve the quality of life for the severely retarded population.

SEXUALITY AND THE PROFOUNDLY MENTALLY RETARDED

In many aspects, the profoundly mentally retarded are much like the severely mentally retarded population, especially when speaking of the group that is multihandicapped and requires twenty-four hour nursing care. For that group, the caregiver encounters the same problems while bathing, and so forth. The only difference is that the level of body, environmental, and self awareness may be lowered even further, especially at an adaptive level.

What does it mean to be profoundly retarded? There is much that is not known about this population because they are usually so low functioning in IQ and adaptive behavior that they are essentially untestable using our current assessment techniques. This is often more evident if the person is also physically handicapped.

Society, unfortunately has just begun to recognize the profoundly mentally retardeds' right to quality of life as individuals. When speaking of quality of life for the profoundly retarded group, it is safe to say that the barest minimum of people would include sexuality as a need. But are they right? Again, it is difficult to know, because there rarely exists an adequate communication system or even a signaling system with this group. These individuals are often limited in communicating their needs for survival, much less their needs or desires for pleasure.

In the profoundly retarded population, self-stimulation of all kinds is evident (see Chapter 9). Along with this, masturbation is often present and in some cases harmful. Nursing care must be good to be sure that fingernails are kept short and that the genitals are not kept red and irritated through the use of proper lotions and medication, if necessary. Objects that could be harmful when masturbating should not be available for use.

The added complication of incontinence, both urinary and bowel can accompany this group. The profoundly retarded are sometimes not toilet trained or toilet scheduled, which means that even as adults they are diapered. If these individuals masturbate when they have urinated or defecated, smearing of feces can occur, as well as many other unsanitary and unhealthy conditions. This is especially difficult with adult females who have their menses and who dig at their genitals during the menstrual time, smearing menstrual blood or attempting to ingest the sanitary pads. Many parents have asked for therapeutic hysterectomies so that the nursing care for these adult women can be more effective. This is something to be considered on an individual basis.

In most homes and some residential facilities, very little programming exists for this population other than *tender loving care*. Therefore, the tendency to *self stimulation* increases. All efforts should be made to provide daily activities of external stimulation that make the environment more interesting. This programming can ensure more awareness of others and not just self for these profoundly retarded individuals.

Because of the severe inability of most of the profoundly retarded to communicate verbally or nonverbally, there is the possibility that caregivers, whether in the home or residential facility, may try to exploit these individuals by masturbating them or taking advantage of them sexually for their own benefit. The mentally retarded individual may not be able to communicate these experiences if they occur. The environment must be very aware and protective of this real possibility.

Example L:

A profoundly retarded multihandicapped adult male was living in a residential facility. On routine examination, the physician found him to have a venereal disease. Further lab work showed that he had gonorrhea. The man was bedridden unless taken out of his bed and put in a wheelchair to go sit in a dayroom and be returned to his private room. He could not talk, walk, feed himself, or meet any of his basic needs.

He clearly was not capable of contracting VD on his own initiative. The assumption of the staff was that either a staff member or visitor with VD had performed fellatio or had sexual intercourse with the man and transmitted the disease. The man was, of course, treated for the VD and was moved from a private room to a ward of four people. Further action could not be taken effectively against anyone, because there was no way to find out who had participated in sex with him.

Just because the profoundly retarded cannot readily participate on a reciprocal level in sexual activity does not mean that they do not enjoy touching and affection. Some of these profoundly retarded people are very tactually defensive because they have never been touched or stroked. It is therefore important for the therapeutic people interacting with them to try and reduce some of this tactual defensiveness by building body and environmental awareness through tactual stimulation. This is not activity that is sexually stimulating, but it does help build contact with the real world and is of great value. All caregivers can be taught to massage effectively, vibrate and rub the face, extremeties, and nongenital areas of the handicapped individual to help with relaxation and general well being. This should be done whenever possible.

There should be an effort made by all not to think of these profoundly limited individuals as nonentities. Possibly it is the adults, the professionals, educators, families, and caregivers who have just not learned yet how to assess and deal with the severe limitations that these people must daily live and cope with themselves.

Everyone should always talk to the profoundly retarded as if they understand. They should treat the most profoundly retarded individual with as much care and respect as the most intelligent individual. Because the person's response level is different, it does not necessarily follow that there is no feeling, need to receive care, or to desire nurture. When sexual expression is exhibited, which will be mostly in the form of masturbation, it should be the caregiver's responsibility to try to make that situation and environment conducive to the person's experimentation. The proviso should exist that the behavior be nonharmful to the individual and is not done in *public*.

Regardless of the level of mental retardation, the individuals involved are and can be sexual. They have the need and right to be. It is the responsibility of the caregivers and society to recognize this. Each person should be approached as an individual, and programs created in environments where everyone is encouraged to live to their fullest potential, regardless of mental or physical handicaps or both. This right is truly all that any one can ask of society — and the mentally retarded should ask no more and receive no less.

chapter three
SEX EDUCATION FOR THE MENTALLY RETARDED

Why is there a need for sex education for the mentally retarded? The majority of society functions on the premise that the mentally retarded are not sexual anyway, or if so, they are very delayed. Many in society feel that the mentally retarded are sterile anyway or cannot understand what you are saying, so why bother with sex education? Society does not do much in this area with the nonmentally retarded population. Hence, why treat the mentally retarded differently? To those who work with the mentally retarded, the answers are so evident that stating them seem oversimplified because we know that delays in developing and retardation in learning and adapting does not make a person asexual.

All people are born sexual and that includes those people who are classified as mentally retarded. They do not learn things as subtly as the nonretarded person in society; therefore, learning strategies must sometimes be more specific and different to meet the needs of this special population. Because the sex education strategy needs to be different does not negate the definite need for the strategy to exist and be developed. It needs to be effective and meaningful. In this way, the mentally retarded may live their lives to their fullest capacity, regardless of their handicaps.

Who then is the most appropriate person or persons to provide this sex education to the mentally retarded individual? As true of any child, the most appropriate learning and easiest learning will take place in the natural environment of the child, usually directed by the caregiving adult in that environment. It, therefore, stands to reason that the most appropriate person to talk to someone about growing up, body changes, maturation, and feelings, is the person closest to the daily living scheme of the individual. The most effective sex education is not done in a classroom but rather occurs in the daily interactions between adults and children. Before removing sex education to the classroom and a technical type setting, all efforts should be made to explore emerging sexuality within the natural living environment of the child.

Professionals lend support systems to these direct caregivers and parents so that they will be more comfortable with their interactions, information-giving, and permission-giving to be sexual. If the classroom is used, generalization techniques are taught so that the knowledge obtained can be useful to the individual in other environments.

ORIENTATION FOR CAREGIVERS

In discussing with caregivers how to do sex education with the mentally retarded, emphasis is placed on the need to start with very basic tenets and move to the more complicated aspects. The programs should keep in mind the cognitive, adaptive, and communicative limitations of the individual who is receiving the sex education.

The retarded individual is assessed for existing knowledge, desire for more knowledge, ability to handle the desired knowledge, and appropriate ways to present the material that will be meaningful and transferable to real life. A female with an I.Q. of 20 does not need verbal information on tubal ligation. However, this person and those caregivers in her environment may well need information and techniques on how to help this adult handle her menses in a nonharmful and sanitary manner through a process of program development to meet specific needs.

On the other hand, a mildly mentally retarded individual, whether male or female, needs specific information about conception, contraception, community resources, veneral disease, parenthood, and marriage. The educational process for teaching sexuality to this group will not differ widely from the nonretarded population, only that the process will take longer, need to be more concrete, and be a repetitive system of delivery of information.

WHO PROVIDES INSTRUCTION?

The actual instruction of sex education can be done by a myriad of people. An important point to remember is that the same material must be delivered with the same language or communication system so that it is consistent and meaningful to the person receiving it. The instructor or giver of information can be school faculty, staff, parents, or a combination of any of these significant adults in the mentally retarded person's environment.

A critical team member is a person who is a qualified programmer in sex education/sex counseling/therapy, as well as in mental retardation. This person determines what is to be taught and the most meaningful way to explore the topics with the retarded population. The point stressed here is to have *qualified* programmers. Unfortunately, there are many who are expert programmers in one or the other of the fields but they do not know how to combine the two fields.

An effective method for utilizing a consultant or staff programmer is to have their special program put on videotapes that can be used in training staff, faculty, and parents. By putting the information on videotapes, material is always available for use in the many training sessions and in discussions afterwards, with the material presented consistently. It is suggested that the sessions be one hour. Thirty minutes should be left to allow for discussion, role playing, or other activities. A pre- and post-attitudinal test on sexuality and the mentally retarded can be administered to see that there is effective communication and personal awareness growth during the training sessions.

A videotape training program was developed by the author for use in training staff and parents of the residents in an institution for the mentally retarded. These tapes have been used in workshops around the country and the author is currently available to provide inservice training workshops which will include the exploration of multimedia. (see Appendix.)

VIDEOTAPE UTILIZATION

Four training sessions are proposed. In the ideal situation, every staff person involved in the setting is required to go through the four hours of training. The total staff participation requirement is based on the premise that sexuality is encountered on a daily basis by everyone who comes into contact with the mentally retarded. If it is a twenty-four hour facility, the program is presented to all three shifts.

The workshops can run four hours consecutively. This is a very heavy dose of sexuality but sometimes the most efficient way to deliver the material, if the lecturer is from out-of-town. Two hours at a time, or one hour per day, probably is preferable, since the groups can have a day inbetween to assimilate and digest the information.

Topics on the tapes are as follows:

Tape I:	Overview of sexuality and the mentally retarded; anatomy and physiology
Tape II:	Birth control and the mentally retarded
Tape III:	Homosexuality, masturbation, wet dreams, fantasies, VD, also dating procedures with the mentally retarded
Tape IIIA:	Sex crimes and the mentally retarded
Tape IV:	Parenthood and marriage with the mentally retarded

The ingredient to success in this kind of audio-visual delivery program is to have a dynamic and qualified group leader who can initiate group discussions and include the audience in role playing at the conclusion of the tapes. Even if the tape material appears sterile or too low keyed to some, the participants can be involved through the group interactive process in the discussions that follow the tapes. The tapes can be effectively used with small or very large groups as long as there is at least one television viewing set for every thirty people in the audience.

GOALS OF TRAINING STAFF

A great deal of desensitization and general awareness of one's own sexuality will be developed during the sessions. It is only when persons become comfortable with their own sexuality that they can be most effective in helping the mentally retarded or anyone else. For that matter, they will become more comfortable with their own sexuality. This fact is to be emphasized to the audience so that they realize the leader's anticipation that they learn about themselves and profit from the information during the inservice tape sessions. Some participants have difficulty with sexual content of the tapes because of strong religious or cultural training that may be anti-masturbation. This can cause conflicts within the staff members if they are working in an environment where masturbation is encouraged as a sexual release and outlet.

MYTHS

It is also important for the participants to realize things such as information that *one can become pregnant through heavy petting without having sexual intercourse.* It is amazing how many adults feel that if you do not have sexual intercourse, you can not get pregnant. Does this sound like such basic information? It is surprising how ignorant of true facts and how much fantasy, myth, and imagination exists when sexuality is discussed. Everyone is influenced by their personal biases, past education and experiences.

The good fortune was not given to most people to learn about themselves sexually through a responsible adult providing appropriate information. Most people at sometime in their education were given accurate information concerning the "trip of the egg down the fallopian tubes." However, feelings are not often discussed. The group inservice training sessions can help accomplish some of this development and shaping of attitudes that make people more able and desirous of dealing with sexuality and the mentally retarded.

DESENSITIZATION TO STREET LANGUAGE

Desensitization to street language and to sex words such as *fuck, screw, cunt, prick, etc.,* is very easy to do. The group leader helps the audience process the words and desensitize to past meanings and connotations. The person develops comfort in hearing the words. Participants will no longer be as shocked or uncomfortable when they hear the words being used by mentally retarded individuals.

The main goal of an inservice videotape program like the one designed and explained here is not to make sex educators or sex counselors of everyone. It is intended to heighten the level of sensitivity and awareness of sexuality in the mentally retarded. This population will then stand a better chance of being accepted as sexual beings. They will be allowed to explore themselves sexually in acceptable and nonharmful ways. It is also an effort to establish consistency in the environment so that all adults are communicating and acting in a similar way with the retarded, providing consistency and thus security. A big step forward is developing a comfort level so that the mentally retarded will be given proper information, be allowed to explore appropriately, and not be punished for being sexual.

DEVELOPING ADMINISTRATIVE SUPPORT

If given the proper guidance and information, many adults can put aside their own prejudices and feelings to help the handicapped cope with this situation. *Administrators* should encourage and support these kinds of sessions. In an institutional setting, success will only come when the *superintendent* and *administration* are directly involved and supportive, even participating in the actual tapes and training sessions. The most important support that can come from the administration is requiring every person, from the groundskeeper to the physicians, to attend and participate in the sessions.

The mentally retarded will go to the person with whom they feel most comfortable to glean the desired information about sex. It will not always be the nurse, houseparent, caregiver, teacher or natural parent. Everyone involved in the daily living schema ought to be willing and prepared with the proper information if the program is to be successful. Everyone should be aware of the societal rules of that environment and the consequences when the rules are not followed so that consistency will be evident and meaningful.

These are the ingredients of a good, successful, and productive program. Everyone involved does not have to *believe* the same way, but everyone has to *react* the same way about sex and sexual behavior or the program's effectiveness will suffer. Without consistency and support of all responsible adults in the environment, it will be difficult to develop these concepts and behaviors in the mentally retarded individuals. Teaching the *ethic of responsibility* in relationship to sexuality and the mentally retarded will be just another fantasy of the administration.

Whether videotapes are used as a vehicle of inservice training or not, there are important considerations when providing sex education with the mentally retarded. These considerations need to be covered in the staff, faculty, or parent training sessions before the material is presented in the actual sex education program with the mentally retarded individual. Winifred Kempton lists the following four points as important considerations in sex education with the mentally retarded:

1. Sex education involves relationships: how we feel about ourselves in relationship to family, friends, lovers, spouses, etc., and how we act according to these feelings.

2. Sex education means learning the physiology of the human body; the respective male and female roles in human

reproduction, and the activity involved.

3. Sex education consists of the understanding of sexual impulses or body feelings (erotic) and how they are aroused and controlled.

4. Differentiate feelings from information.[1]

MATERIALS

People who are trained in sex education/sex counseling with nonretarded populations but have limited experience with the retarded must recognize the need for *extreme concreteness* of language when working with the mentally retarded. *Abstraction* in language ability develops slowly and sometimes not at all. Materials developed and used should emphasize low-level language words, augmentative/alternative communication modes where applicable (e.g., sign language, language boards, picture boards, Blissymbolics, prosthetic speech devices).

If pictures are used, they should be clear, concise drawings, easily explained, and color coded for explicity. (refer to Pragmatics of Colored Chalk in the Appendix.)

SOCIAL BEHAVIOR

Social behavior and all of its interactive processes from learning to greet people, developing conversational skills, sharing social experiences, and so forth, need to be discussed and developed. Time should be spent on how to teach the mentally retarded to have a good time with others in a social milieu that is not sexual in nature. The mentally retarded need to learn how to enjoy same-sex or opposite-sex experiences that are affectionate in nature but do not culminate in sexual intercourse.

TECHNIQUES — FOLLOW THROUGH AND PRACTICE

Regardless of the discussion or the focus of training, the responsible adult should always use repetition and get feedback from the mentally retarded individual to make sure they understand the content and meaning of what has been discussed. The mentally retarded must be able to apply it to their daily living schema or it will be useless.

Well trained and appropriate programmers need to establish programs and situations where the mentally retarded people can practice the skills that have been taught and thus develop some age-appropriate socialization behavior that is fun oriented, interactive, but nonsexual in nature. It is then that a decrease in sexual behavior that is unacceptable to the environment may be noticed.

In the inservice training programs, caregiving and professional adults respond very positively to role playing techniques; this is found to also be true with the mentally retarded. At first the males and females can role play separately and then together beginning with familiar situations and the behavior observed and generated by those situations, and then moving to role playing of appropriate versus inappropriate behavior. Such an approach has proven extremely effective in helping the mentally retarded establish and maintain the concept of *who is responsible* and what is *appropriate and inappropriate.* It is important not to label behaviors as either *"good"* or *"bad,"* but rather *appropriate or inappropriate* — especially in relationship to the environment in which the professional is working.

As sex education is provided, an important factor to communicate to adults in the inservice training programs and then to the mentally retarded themselves is that they have the human privilege or right to express themselves sexually. There is a need to inform the mentally retarded of societal biases and any existing laws or rules that exist in the environment in which they live. All of this should be done within the perspective of how to react to these laws or rules, if there are feelings that it is unfair to an innate right to express sexuality. Advocacy offices for the handicapped should be opened and made accessible to the mentally retarded.

In her many publications, Winifred Kempton, one of the forerunners and leaders of sexuality and the mentally retarded, developed many techniques and procedures that are effective in sex education/sex counseling with the mentally retarded. Refer to the Bibliography and Related Interests material to obtain more information on Mrs. Kempton's work.

RESOURCES

Anyone beginning a sexuality program for the mentally retarded should look carefully at the available resources to see what is useable for their situation. Knowing what has succeeded and what has failed for others is often helpful in designing and developing meaningful programming. A bibliography, including related materials, and appendix is included at the end of this book.

One sure way to fail in a sex education program for the mentally retarded is to start at a level that is too high cognitively for the individual. This is why the traditionally trained sex educator from a health department has difficulty in working with the mentally retarded. It is important to understand the adaptive behavior, learning abilities, limitations, and styles of the people the programmer is attempting to educate.

Example A:
Staff in a residential facility had requested sex education for three moderately retarded female adolescents who were beginning to show an interest in boys. They were taken downtown to the sex educator's office, where she methodically took out materials gleaned from other sources. One resource said to administer a test to see exactly what information the mentally retarded person already had about sexuality, and if they did not have the ability to read, the test should be given orally. That seemed easy enough. None of these girls could read well, so the sex educator proceeded to individually take the girls into her office to ask the questions. Typical questions were "Do you know what a vagina is? What is sexual intercourse? What are sperm?"

On the surface, these questions sound so very simple. In reality, to an institutionalized female who has had no background in this terminology, the questions meant nothing. Blank stares or "I don't know" were the consistent answers received. It took about five minutes per girl for the sex educator to realize that the tool she had chosen was totally inappropriate. The sex educator realized it was time to put all gathered material aside, approach each girl as an individual, try to find out what they knew, and proceed. The truth was that the girls had no accurate information but were willing to learn. A simple chalkboard and colored chalk (see Appendix for Pragmatics of Colored Chalk) was used to help develop the concept of imparting information that was useful and meaningful to the girls in their environment. Had the sex educator been rigid and proceeded with the program chosen from the stack of gathered literature, there would have been immediate failure.

Sex education for the mentally retarded takes a great deal of creativity and flexibility. Each mentally retarded individual deserves to be met as a person with their own merits, needs, and abilities. A good programmer will be able to identify and work in this manner. The providing of information and counseling about feelings should be consistent within the environment, but it should be recognized that there will always be someone who has more skill at doing the actual sex education/sex counseling than others. This person or persons should be used wisely and effectively.

Example B:
It is difficult to have just one person who is available and competent to do the sex education/sex counseling with the mentally retarded within a special environment. Therefore, the experienced sex educator/sex counselor programmer should always attempt to include someone from the mentally retarded individual's daily environment in the sessions. In that way the adult can learn how to follow through on what is being taught. This will heighten the ability of the other significant people in the mentally retarded person's environment so that they will deal with sex education on a daily basis.

It has been found that once these other significant adults are included in several sex education or sex counseling sessions, two things will happen: (1) the other adults will assume more responsibility for completing the programming without calling the "so-called" expert every time there is a question or a problem, (2) the mentally retarded person will be able to identify another person in the living environment with whom it is all right to discuss problems concerning sexuality and will begin to use this person as a resource.

Example C:
A sex educator and physician went to a group of teenage male mild and moderately mentally retarded individuals to provide sex education. The physician was very open and started drawing very real life type diagrams on the chalkboard. The physican also was writing out the proper terminology names by the parts of anatomy. There was very poor attention to what was happening in the session. The sex educator sensed that something was wrong as the mentally retarded did not seem interested and so the men were asked to read the words being written on the chalkboard. Not one person in the group could read the words. After this vivid example of being at too high a level, the team leaders tried to regroup and erased the

terminology. This helped some. Unfortunately the stage had already been set. The mentally retarded men felt inferior and inadequate and were no longer receptive.

The leaders of a sex education group should make it their business to know ahead of time what the learning abilities and cognitive levels of the individuals are before the sessions begin so that these kinds of errors can be avoided.

Example D:
Often the mentally retarded are shy when they are suddenly confronted with a situation where it is all right to talk about something that has always been off-limits. They will not ask questions or venture forth verbally. When working with this type of group, it is useful to have two adults leading the group. They can take turns assuming the role of student and teacher in role playing situations and they can ask some of the questions that the mentally retarded individuals may be too scared or embarrassed to ask. Once the flow of questions and answers begins, the mentally retarded individuals will usually join in, giving their own experiences and asking their own questions.

SUMMARY

Basically, in planning a sexuality training program for the mentally retarded that includes sex education/sex counseling and/or sex therapy, several things are imperative:

1. Policies need to be developed and supported by the administration and communicated to the parents as well as to all caregivers and professionals working with the mentally retarded group.

2. Everyone involved with the mentally retarded person needs to assume some responsibility for at least feeling comfortable enough with their own sexuality so that they can deal with the sexuality of others.

3. Any dating rules or standards expected for appropriate social behavior in an environment should be clearly communicated to all and enforced by everyone involved.

4. Using videotapes as an inservice training device that keeps material consistent is an excellent tool. This technique allows for

personal interchange and role playing around feelings in response to the material or the tapes.

5. It is imperative that the sexuality programming is given by someone experienced both in sex education/sex counseling/sex therapy and also in mental retardation. This ensures that there is good comprehension of both fields.

6. Without good administrative support, well informed staff, faculty, parents, and a qualified programmer there will be no adequate sexuality program for the mentally retarded. All of the above must exist to make the significant impact that is needed.

Footnote
[1] Kempton, W. *Sex education for persons with disabilities that hinder learning: A teacher's guide.* Philadelphia, PA: Planned Parenthood, 1980.

chapter four

SUBJECT AREAS
TO BE COVERED
IN SEX EDUCATION

It has been stated earlier that the person providing sex education with the mentally retarded should be aware of the level of retardation and the learning style of the recipient of the knowledge. This should always be kept in mind as the specific program for an individual is developed. All programming should be individualized as much as possible. Basic information should be imparted at whatever level is possible for the retarded person to comprehend and process in a meaningful way. It is important for the sex educator to be aware of the language level of the individual in the program and to adjust the material as necessary.

When developing staff and parent training tapes or programs, it is necessary to cover general topics and certain information under each topic. This is also true when working with the mentally retarded individual. There are some basic areas that deserve identification and consideration at this point. They are the following:

1. Anatomy and physiology

2. Maturation/body changes

3. Birth control

4. Venereal Disease

5. Masturbation

6. Responsibility of being sexual

7. Same-sex and opposite-sex behavior

8. Psychosocial-sexual behavior

9. Parenthood and marriage

This chapter will take each of these nine subheadings and briefly outline basic information that should be included in developing an appropriate and meaningful program for the mentally retarded. The following outline style is used for clarity and easy access as *reference* or *resource* points.

Anatomy and Physiology
— Use simple drawing of males and females (see Pragmatics of Colored Chalk in Appendix).
— Indicate similarities and differences in males and females.
— Use proper medical terminology for genitals; respond to current street language being used, if any; try to exchange it for appropriate medical terminology.
— Make sure that the males understand female anatomy and the females understand male anatomy.
— Teach that the genitals are *private* body parts and need to be treated as private.
— Emphasize that males and females come in different shapes, sizes, and colors.
— Stress that everyone has the same body parts but they may very in shape, size, etc.

Maturation/Body Changes
— Refer to anatomy, show development of body from birth to maturity.
— Help the mentally retarded relate to their own body as it is today, was before, and will be at maturity.
— Teach necessary behavior and self-help skills that are necessary for females to handle: menstruation, body odor, vaginal discharge, hair growth on pubic area and underarms, and legs, wearing of appropriate underclothing such as bras, etc., care of genitals. For males, the appropriate grooming techniques of shaving, elimination of body odor, care of genitals, wet dreams, erections (nocturnal and regular), and how to clean ejaculate after wet dreams or masturbation.
— Give information that is appropriate and necessary to the opposite sex so that they can understand information they may hear from the opposite sex or experience in an encounter, i.e., males should know about the process of maturation of the females and the females should know about the maturation of

the males.
— Discuss the feelings that accompany maturation and body changes.
— Emphasize the mentally retarded individual's responsibility for dealing with the feelings involved in being sexual.
— Discuss outlets for the feelings which include masturbation. This is a good time to lead into a discussion of masturbation.
— Refer to information on anatomy and physiology, noting that all nine areas are intertwined. There is not a specific need for approaching the presentation in any set, formal way or order. The material should be presented to best meet the needs of the individual or group.

Birth Control
— Give basic information about conception and contraception.
— Explain function of ovum and sperm (refer to Pragmatics of Colored Chalk in Appendix).
— Explain how a baby is formed and where it is housed in mother's body.
— Show simple diagrams of contraception.
— Show the actual birth control devices that are appropriate for this session, i.e., condoms, foam, diaphragm, IUD, birth control pills, etc.
— Use drawings to discuss sterilization both in males and females as options for birth control.
— Talk about the responsibility of both partners to practice birth control.
— Emphasize the necessity of both partners being aware of how to use the different birth control items such as the condom, i.e., females should know how to purchase condoms, put them on the males, and remove them properly.
— Explain where birth control can be obtained in the community, i.e., what requires a doctor's help such as sterilization, birth control pills, IUD's, and what is readily available at drugstore or other stores, i.e., condoms, foams, suppositories, etc.
— Explain specific knowledge about when different birth control methods need to be employed, i.e., the pill must be taken regularly whether the person is being active sexually or not, but the foam or condom should be used before each act of intercourse and not after the act of intercourse.
— Emphasize that no birth control will be effective unless used properly.
— Discuss community resources, such as family planning clinics,

where free birth control can be obtained, as well as information on birth control for both males and females.
— Give information on abortions; what they are, how they can be legally obtained, who has to pay for them, and general cost in terms of both money and health.
— Explain that abortions are used as a method of birth control by some people.
— Emphasize what birth control usually is most effective with the mentally retarded. Spend less time on information which will be esoteric to this population or difficult for them to effectively use.
— Check with public health officials to be sure that the most currently available information is provided.
— Give pragmatic information on birth control that is specifically appropriate to the situation and the individuals involved. Overall general information should also be dispersed.

Venereal Disease
— Define venereal disease and give the different symptoms of the most common venereal disease such as syphillis, gonorrhea, and herpes. Provide signs that the individual can identify in a partner before having sexual contact, so that the likelihood of contracting venereal disease is decreased.
— Explain danger signals to spot on one's own body that require medical examination.
— Discuss where and how to get that examination, and how can it be obtained free if there are no money resources.
— Explain condoms as protection against venereal disease.
— Discuss health problems encountered if venereal disease is left untreated.
— General methods of treatment once venereal disease is diagnosed

Masturbation
— Give definition (refer to Chapter 9).
— Explain how males and females masturbate — similarities and differences.
— Discuss appropriate environmental settings for masturbation.
— Emphasize that masturbation is a private act.
— Explain mutual masturbation by the same-sex and opposite-sex.
— Discuss masturbation as foreplay to sexual intercourse.
— Explain masturbation can result in pregnancy. Explain that

sperm can enter the vagina causing fertilization and pregnancy through intercourse or through masturbation when ejaculate is on hands or near vagina (sperm able to enter even though no intercourse has taken place).

— Discuss feelings about masturbation; handling feelings, and the feelings and responses of people in the environment.
— Explore positive and negative feelings.
— Explain nonharmful ways to masturbate.
— Explain harmful ways to masturbate.

Responsibility of Being Sexual
— Ask, "Is everybody sexual?"
— Ask, "Who is responsibile for oneself and one's body?"
— Discuss how to help the mentally retarded accept that they are responsible for their own bodies, sexuality, and sexual behavior.
— Explore understanding concepts and processes of responsibility, appropriateness, inappropriateness, problem solving around sexual encounters, and how to act upon feelings in a responsible way.
— Emphasize that it is all right to say "No" and how to say "No."
— Ask who is responsibile for saying "Yes" or "No"?
— If sexual behavior is exhibited, the mentally retarded have to assume the responsibilities that accompany being sexual, e.g., birth control, family planning, etc.
— Explore understanding restrictions of certain living environments, learning to live within these restrictions and making adjustments to the environments so that the rules are easier and more acceptable to the individual.
— Discuss responsibility for following society's rules and laws governing sexual behavior in certain environments.
— Explain ways to use advocacy programming to change rules and laws that are felt to be unfair or unconstitutional.

Same-Sex and Opposite-Sex Behavior
— Differentiate between heterosexual and homosexual behavior and explain how during adolescence this might better be referred to as same-sex or opposite-sex behavior. Relate this to the fact that definitive gender preferences and life choices have not been made in most cases.
— Explain discovery of sexual self and others usually involves same-sex and/or opposite-sex behavior, involving

responsibilities and response patterns.
— Discuss benefits and problems encountered in experiencing both same-sex and opposite-sex behavior.
— Explore ability of the mentally retarded person to evaluate and work within existing structures of society.

PSYCHOSOCIAL-SEXUAL BEHAVIOR

— Explain appropriate and inappropriate behaviors.
— Discuss relationship to many different enviornments.
— Emphasize the importance of adapting and differentiating when psychosocial-sexual behavior should be exhibited and is acceptable.
— Explore societal rules, laws, and expectations.
— Explain where and how to get counseling and help in adjusting to societal demands.
— Discuss use of community resources whenever feasible and possible.
— Explore appropriate psychosocial-sexual behavior for different situations such as parties, dances, dates to the movies.
— Explore the entire scope of dating and courtship.
— Discuss pros and cons of playing the dating game.
— Emphasize the absolute requirement of understanding the meaning of involvement with someone who is under legal age.
— Detail different state laws pertaining to legal age and relevance of the laws to the individual.
— Discuss the way society controls inappropriate social-sexual behavior in the community, i.e., consequences of inappropriate behavior.
— Discuss consenting partners.
— Explore privacy and rights to privacy.
— Explain statutory rape.
— Explain indecent exposure.
— Discuss feelings surrounding the act of being labelled mentally retarded in a social environment and how to respond.
— Explore taking advantage of community resources for recreation and learning to be part of the handicapped and nonhandicapped community.
— Detail techniques to ensure good productive and meaningful use of leisure time.

Parenthood and Marriage
— Explore laws prohibiting marriage in 38 states — how to accept

this or fight it through the courts and advocacy programs.
— Discuss responsibilities and pragmatics of entering into parenthood and/or marriage, i.e., what coping skills, technical skills, financial skills, and resources are necessary to cope in society.
— Explore the support systems that exist in the community or within families to help the mentally retarded with the prospect of parenthood and/or marriage.
— Discuss consideration of marriage without parenthood, i.e., sterilization and how to have it done.
— Suggest actual experiences in baby sitting, living independently, developing appropriate and necessary communication skills, running a household, and budgeting.
— Develop reality oriented support structure from the adults to help the retarded couple assess what aspects of parenthood and marriage they are ready for or interested in; set goals for learning this knowlege.
— Develop awareness that one can be a fulfilled and happy individual (including sexual fulfillment) without either parenthood or marriage.

In working directly with the mentally retarded individual, the sex educator will see the need to further reduce some of the information. The sex educator should make as much of an effort as possible to make the sessions as individually appropriate as possible, thus building a more realistic and possible avenue for the person to use in growing towards developing sexuality.

It should be reiterated that each person, regardless of level of mental retardation and adaptive functioning, needs to be clinically and thereapeutically treated as an individual, with all innate personal rights being respected.

chapter five

THE PURPOSE AND ROLE OF SEX COUNSELING WITH THE MENTALLY RETARDED

PRIMARY PURPOSE

The main purpose of providing sex counseling for the mentally retarded is to help them assume responsibility for their own sexuality. The sex counseling experience is more than just information giving and assurance of comprehension. The person providing the sex counseling should be experienced both in counseling and human sexuality, as well as being experienced in counseling a mentally retarded population.

SOCIETAL INPUT

Historically, society has generally not considered the mentally retarded as responsible persons and has not expected or demanded responsible behavior from them. In contrast, certain portions of society have taken away rights to marriage, privacy, and so forth that would indicate a person's capacity to be responsible. It is up to the mentally retarded to prove through responsible behavior that they are not only entitled to the rights of others in society but that they can handle the responsibility inherent in those roles.

ROLE OF SEX COUNSELOR

In achieving this responsibility, the sex counselor can be a most influential person in the lives of these mentally retarded people. A basic assumption of all sex counseling is that the mentally retarded are capable of being responsible for their own bodies, emerging sexuality, and sexual selves.

How does this differ or appear similar to the previous chapter on sex education for the mentally retarded? The main similarity is that the sex counselor has the perfect opportunity to reinforce the information given in sex education and should use this to the best advantage to help the mentally retarded achieve maximum growth and understanding of human sexuality.

As with sex education, sex counseling can be either provided in individual or group sessions. There is much positive to be said for group counseling because peer pressure and interaction can be a powerful force in helping the mentally retarded achieve standards of appropriate behavior for their environment.

DIFFERENCES BETWEEN SEX COUNSELING AND SEX EDUCATION

The main difference between sex counseling and sex education is the emphasis on feelings versus information. Sex counseling probes towards feelings. Sex counseling uses techniques of role playing and psychotherapy to help the mentally retarded develop some of the inner thoughts and problems involved in feeling sexual, being mentally retarded, and the complications these feelings have in the eyes of society.

The role of the sex counselor is to explore feelings and behaviors in the counseling sessions with the mentally retarded. It is important to understand that the behavior is affected by handicaps, in addition to being governed and influenced by the rules and attitudes of society in which the person lives. An appropriate sex counseling concept to impart is that the mentally retarded should feel and behave as *adults with handicaps* rather than *handicapped adults*, especially in relationship to developing sexuality, sexual feelings about self, and sexual feelings about others.

EMPHASIS OF SEX COUNSELING SESSIONS

The sex counseling sessions should emphasize surfacing feelings and respond to them as feelings rather than just information or knowledge that is acquired. For movement and resolution to occur the mentally retarded must emote and function at a feeling level. This can best be achieved once the information is received and processed on a solid, concrete, and meaningful level.

Sex counseling with the mentally retarded usually is done in a verbal mode/communication type program. For those individuals who are nonverbal or who use alternative/augmentative modes of communication, such as sign language, language boards, prosthetic speech devices, the sex counselor should be familiar with the communicative processes needed to provide the sex counseling.

One of the most effective tools to use in sex counseling is role playing. Psychotherapeutic dynamics can be used as proposed by proponents of role playing dynamics in the psychotherapy literature.

The sex counselor should take personal counseling experience with nonretarded individuals and adapt the techniques and procedures in such a way that they are meaningful and comprehensible to the mentally retarded individual. The qualified sex counselor need only increase knowledge and understanding of mental retardation. Once this competency level in mental retardation is secure, the sex counseling program will be well on the way to becoming meaningful and enriching.

The sex counselor should also be aware of the procedures and policies of the state and federal government, regarding rights to privacy and the interpretation of these rights for specific environments. The sex counselor can be effective by involving advocacy programs to ensure that the rights of the mentally retarded are not being abused.

ACHIEVING THE LEAST RESTRICTIVE ENVIRONMENTS

Whenever possible, the sex counselor should help the mentally retarded live in the least restrictive environment possible. Obviously, this is the kind of environment where unrestricted sexual expression will be tolerated better. Anyone capable of living independently should be encouraged to do so and to be responsible for their total behavior and performance. The sex counselor can be an important person in the preparation process for the mentally retarded to move into the community on an independent basis and can continue to provide a support program for the person.

At this point, all responsible sex counseling with the mentally retarded should be done in a verbal, (or appropriate augmentative/alternative communication mode) style, using acceptable psychotherapeutic techniques. Any hands-on teaching is taboo and probably will remain so for quite some time (refer to

Chapter 9). The public at large does not appear ready to handle what to do when the mentally retarded are *sexually dysfunctional*, as the public has not yet admitted that the retarded are *sexual*. This is literally a topic that will be extremely difficult because of the courts and parents' tendencies to perpetually infantilize the mentally retarded, and the shouts and screams of the morality groups. The topic of sexuality is difficult for most people to accept. Admitting that the area of sex counseling should also include the population of the mentally retarded is a new concept.

The mentally retarded, historically, have been thought of as nonsexual and, at the most, thought to need only enough information to understand maturational changes in their bodies. Everyone has ignored the feelings that accompany these changes, whether the mentally retarded person can verbalize them or not. It will take time to develop the concept of sex counseling as a viable tool and effective avenue for the mentally retarded. The end goal is to help the mentally retarded achieve fuller and more complete lives in general, becoming more responsible sexually, at the specific level appropriate for the individual.

chapter six
LIVING ENVIRONMENTS

The sex counselor ought to be aware of and familiar with the different living environments available to the mentally retarded person in the community. The sex counselor should then explore the individual client's specific needs in this area.

Different living environments require adaptation to the limitations of behavior inherent to the situation. There is a clear correlation that the more restrictive a living environment, the more probable it will be to find constrictions on sexual expression and behavior. The main question and point to consider is restrictive to whom? To one mentally retarded individual, a residential facility may be the least restrictive environment and offer the most opportunity for socialization and expression of self, including sexuality. To another mentally retarded individual, the natural home, or independently living in the community might be the least restrictive.

There are many easy and clear examples of sexual limitations placed on persons living in certain areas. For example, a mentally retarded individual living at home will usually neither be encouraged nor allowed to participate sexually with a sibling or family member, thus making the opportunity restrictive for the development of sexual expression.

On the other hand, the individual living in a state facility may have to abide by archaic and rigid laws that are biased and that remove the constitutional rights to privacy. Still, these people have the daily opportunity to meet, greet, socialize, and relate to other peers. Even if sexual relating is against the rules, there will still be many opportunities for peer interaction. In this case, the residential facility may be the least restrictive environment for that person.

The definition of restrictive versus least restrictive in relationship to sexual expression must be considered on an individual basis. The statement cannot be made that just because someone is in a residential facility, that is the most restrictive environment. Indeed, the opposite may be true.

Mentally retarded persons encouraged to live independently in the community before developing the skills necessary to cope with community life may break the laws because they lack the internal control systems necessary to modify behavior. They may become incarcerated and thus, by being in jail, be in the most restrictive environment.

The specific abilities and limitations of the mentally retarded individual should be considered when determining what makes an environment restrictive. Once external restrictions are conquered, such as making sure that there are ramps for wheelchairs, the internal restrictions of coping skills and adaptive levels of the mentally retarded person should be studied by the professionals making the decision. The *feelings* of the mentally retarded person should always be considered within the scope of *reality*. Just because a mentally retarded person wants to live independently does not necessarily mean that person should be encouraged to do so, if the coping skills have not yet been developed.

It is important to counsel the mentally retarded to see if they have the capability to move from one living environment to another. If certain criterion levels are necessary for the process, they should be made clear to the individual. Simple easy processes should be established that will enable them to move through the process from restrictive to least restrictive.

CHOICES OF LIVING ENVIRONMENTS WITH INHERENT SEXUAL PROBLEMS AND RESTRICTIONS

Living Independently in the Community

Many mentally retarded, predominantly at the mild and high moderate levels, consider the ultimate to be living independently in the community. In preparation for this move, parents and programmers emphasize budgeting, food shopping and preparation, nutritional counseling, danger situations, and how to get help. However, not many professionals and parents take the time and energy to prepare the young mentally retarded adult to live sexually in the community — perhaps in an environment where casual sex is the accepted milieu, VD is prevalent, and the mentally retarded are prey of prostitutes and pimps, both heterosexuals and homosexuals.

What is appropriate knowledge about birth control and family planning clinics? This is as important as the mentally retarded person knowing where to go when there is pain or an earache. Who addresses this knowledge, introduces the mentally retarded person to the community facilities, and offers follow up services? If more of this were provided, it would be more realistic to expect some of the higher level, mentally retarded individuals to make the transition successfully into independently living in the community.

The reality is that there are thousands, if not millions, of people already living and coping in the community-at-large who would score within the mentally retarded range on an IQ test, if tested. If so, why can not the people who have been identified by the professionals as mentally retarded, but have had the benefit of proper programming, also live in the community? Maybe, once there is recognition of the true abilities of the higher level mentally retarded to function and to cope in a sexual way, there will be more acceptance for their being able to behave sexually in the community in independent living environments.

Living Independently in a Boarding Home
Many mentally retarded people have the desire and ability to live alone or with a partner, as long as there is minimal supervision available. A boarding home run by someone who will offer minimal support in the areas of counseling, financial affairs, use of community resources, and compliance with appropriate behavior and social standards for the community will make it easier for the mentally retarded to live in this situation.

Many boarding homes will not be coeducational. However, possibility of a coeducational boarding home does exist. The mentally retarded invididual has to be properly prepared by family and programmers to live with someone of the opposite sex and to accept the responsibilities that accompany this type of heterosexual relationship. There might also be a homosexual relationship. The individual has to be aware of community responses to this type of relationship and the consequences imposed by society when one makes this choice.

The rules and restrictions that exist in the boarding home should be made clear so that they can best adjust themselves to comply. Behavior which is often appropriate to one environment and situation will be found to be inappropriate in another situation. This needs to be defined clearly and communicated to the mentally retarded.

Many boarding homes will not have curfews stating when the boarders must return at night. Although the boarder may not be able to entertain someone of the opposite sex at home, living in this less restrictive environment does provide the opportunity to choose the time for returning. In turn, this allows visits to other persons' private homes or explortions of community facilities for a sexual experience. By living in a boarding home, there can be supervision for some of the basic daily needs and a great deal of freedom to explore sexuality within the community-at-large, even though the boarding home, specifically, might be restrictive.

Living in a Supervised Apartment Complex

This arrangement could be very beneficial for the mildly retarded couple, married or not, who choose to live together but need minimal supervision in handling the activities of daily living. In this kind of environment, someone is available to troubleshoot in problem areas. In relationship to sexuality, this supervisor should be aware of community resources for sex education/sex counseling/sex therapy, birth control, family planning, and diagnosis and treatment of venereal disease.

Ideally, this supervisory individual is also open and responsive to discussing sexuality, the emergence of feelings about relationships, and communications that breakdown relationships. This person should be able to act as the giver of information concerning basic experiences and feelings in sexuality so that the mentally retarded living in the apartments will have an adequate support system in force.

In setting up this kind of supervised apartment complex, it would be very beneficial for the supervisor to have some inservice training in the above areas from someone experienced in sexuality and the mentally retarded. The inservice provider could remain as a resource to the supervisor to help in any developing problems.

Living in Group Homes or Half-way Houses

Group homes and half-way houses can be either same-sexed or coeducational. In either situation, the rules and policies concerning sexual behavior need to be developed by administration and communicated definitively and appropriately to the clients.

These homes are usually heavily staffed twenty-four hours a day and are supervised living situations. As such, they do not allow for much sexual expression between two people. There is a lack of privacy. These homes are also usually state operated and comply with state laws prohibiting sexual intercourse between unmarried persons.

Most group homes do, however, give the residents the

opportunity to sign themselves out for specific amounts of time. It is during these time periods, that many of these residents will choose to have sexual encounters. When this is occurring, the staff should be sure that the clients have the appropriate information necessary to deal with the emotions and pragmatic aspects of their behavior. This information includes using birth control, being aware of venereal disease, avoiding pimps, prostitutes, and dangerous situations.

Community resources, especially in the area of family planning, should be used by the community home staffs. Within the group home or half-way house itself, all efforts should be made to engage the clients in appropriate social activities with minimal supervision which will help them function at a more independent level in the community at a later date.

Privacy is stressed. Masturbation, when done alone in the privacy of the bedroom or bathroom should be encouraged. The group home or half-way house usually has fewer people assigned to one bedroom, thus making privacy for masturbation a little easier to achieve.

Residing in a Family Home or an Extended Family Home
The very liberal family who wishes their mentally retarded offspring to have sexually fulfilling experiences may have to assume the responsibility of housing. They can establish the foundation and rules that will allow or disallow certain sexual behavior in the home, either while married or unmarried. This would be done the same way it was done with nonretarded siblings.

When parents are not able to or willing to do this, there may be a sibling or other extended family member who can offer this support system. Possibly a small mobile home could be placed on family property where the mentally retarded couple could live independently but with as much support and supervision as is required.

At any rate, the family members need to do more than just give permission for sexual activity. They ought to be ready to support through community interaction any of the necessary components for sexuality training or counseling that are needed. The family members should feel and be open with the couple about sexual behavior, its benefits and consequences, especially in relationship to birth control. If not, a pregnancy may result when that was not the intent of condoning the expression of sexuality.

It should be remembered that the mentally retarded may not

always acquire the small nuances of sexuality and sexual responsibility through the mass media. The mentally retarded population has to be approached and taught individually. Almost any interested party can learn how to fulfill this role.

Residential Placement in a State or Private Facility
Because of the lack of privacy and the encumberance of laws that are restrictive to personal choice and expression, the institutionalized mentally retarded will usually have the most restrictive environment with respect to sexual feeling and sexual expression.

The institution may have the recreational staff to provide some of the best socialization activities and the most overall *fun* at the *social*. However, the institution probably will be the place that has the most rigid and restrictive rules and regulations regarding sexual expression, especially concerning sexual intercourse.

The time is fast approaching when most institutions will be facilities for the severely and profoundly retarded. All other mentally retarded people will be housed in one of the other above mentioned living environments which have more flexibility about sexual expression.

The least that the institution can do is to have a good overall sex education/sex counseling program that aims at informing all staff members of the sexual needs and rights of the mentally retarded and the administrative rules and regulations of the facility. There should also be a specially designated person trained in sexuality and mental retardation to be a resource for the staff and clients to insure that the above is being implemented properly.

Therefore, the decision needs, as always, to be a very individualized one. It should be emphasized that a mentally retarded person can move from one level to another in a positive sense, finding the place that is most comfortable in which to live and function.

VALID QUESTIONS ON THE ISSUE

Do the Mentally Retarded Have the Ability and Should They Have the Permission to Make Living Arrangement Choices?
Test results and analysis of behavior by professionals and programmers familiar with the mentally retarded individual should be available when they meet to decide what the chances for

success are in each of the different living environments. There are no guarantees. But the acquisition of compliant and adaptive behaviors will increase the likelihood of success in certain living situations.

Permission to make the choice is another matter. If the mentally retarded individual has not been adjudicated incompetent by the court system and is of legal age in that particular state, then the individual has the right. The family or state would have to petition the state through the court system to prove incompetency before taking away the right. (refer to Chapter 10 on legal issues.)

As stated previously, each mentally retarded individual should be assessed and counseled as individually as possible in a clinical and therapeutic sense. However, pragmatically, it becomes necessary to consider characteristics common to certain groups of the mentally retarded population. It should always be recognized that there will be overlap and exceptions to any set of criterion that is used. Flexibility on the part of the professional ensures protection of the individual.

It is important to differentiate between different levels of mental retardation. This is an obvious statement that needs to be made. It is common knowledge that the mildly retarded should certainly be able to actively participate in the choice of a living environment. The individual also should be able to hire an advocate to help in a fight in the court system if family members and professionals try to take the right of choice away from them.

As the levels of retardation get lower some questions will arise. For example, the moderately retarded with appropriate communication skills should be able to adequately survive in a well supervised group home or half-way house where there is sufficient programming. These people should be given the chance to actively participate in the choice of a move to an environment such as this. Possibly the choice can best be made by giving the individual the opportunity to spend several weekends and vacations in the new environment. These visits will let professionals have a better chance to measure and assess coping skills for dealing with the new environment before the actual move is taken.

Should There Be Coeducational Living Environments?
The desired answer for this question is an emphatic "yes." It is recognized that this will only work with an open, liberal staff and community that will be able to deal openly with developing sexuality and possible heterosexual or homosexual expressions or relationships. The staff will have to be willing to channel the energy

and sexual interests of the clients in such a way that they exhibit behavior compatible with the societal rules that the group or half-way home has adopted regarding mutual masturbation and sexual intercourse. When this channeling can be done effectively, a very positive environment can be provided for the mildly retarded in a coeducational group home or half-way house.

For those professionals who feel discomfort with the concept, there is no need for condoning overt sexual behavior. There should be a great deal of encouragement for the development of appropriate and meaningful relationships. This could lead the staff towards helping the couple move to a less restrictive environment. If a couple desired to be sexually active and it was against the rules of the community home, the staff programming responsibility would be to work towards appropriate movement into a less restrictive environment. This move would occur after the programmers decide that the mentally retarded individual or couple can handle it responsibly.

This process can easily be tested in a coeducational living environment. There should be no problem in having a coeducational living environment within a society that has rules restricting sexual intercourse. The programmers are in a position to make a professional judgment that the couple involved are ready to make a mature and competent decision. Further, that they can handle a relationship which includes the emotional and physical aspects of sexual intercourse. It then becomes the responsibility of the staff or programmers to help the couple find and adjust to an alternate living arrangement that allows this sexual expression.

Is There a Double or Triple Standard?

Unfortunately, considering a family home versus a group home versus a residential facility, different standards of allowed and encouraged sexual behavior will be found. This is partly due to puritanical ethics, religious beliefs by some groups, double standards, archaic laws that need rewriting and challenging, and a myriad of other circumstances.

However, it is unrealistic to think that the world will change all at once. The most effective role to take as an advocate would be to assess whether there were an unconstitutional bias being taken towards the mentally retarded because of their place or habitat. If true, the courts could be approached through the advocacy program. The constitutional law and right to privacy (refer to legal aspects of Chapter 10) should help to obliterate the double or triple standard that does exist. This will be a slow process; but if never begun, even on the smallest scale, it will surely never be achieved at any level.

Are Mentally Retarded Able To Change Adaptive Behavior To Accommodate and Comply With Rules That Change From One Environment To Another?

This is a most valid question. As has been stated in this book and many others, the area of adaptive behavior is one in which the mentally retarded have significant difficulty. In fact, it is one of the reasons that these individuals were labeled *mentally retarded* in the first place.

Therefore, assessment has to determine if the mentally retarded individual has the ability to develop the necessary adaptive behavior required to be successful in the new, less restrictive living environment. If so, training can begin. This assessment should be decided by professionals, programmers, family members, and the individual.

When there is doubt, a trial period of adjustment can still be offered. There must be the understanding that if the person is not successful in the less restrictive environment, there should be a return to an environment with more supervision. Specific guidelines in regards to sexual behavior should be presented so that the likelihood of compliance will be enhanced. This experience should aim at being a positive one, even if it is not successful. With more growth and instruction, other attempts at movement can be made later.

PSYCHOSOCIAL-SEXUAL RULES

Application of Rules to the Mentally Retarded

There are many implied and direct psychosocial-sexual rules that are evident as expectations from society. The two basic responses by society are the following:

1. It is implied that the *mentally retarded should not be sexual.* This is easily seen by the constant infantalization of the mentally retarded by family members and society both. Each faction has difficulty understanding that people with adult bodies have adult sexual needs, regardless of their mentality, and that sexual desire usually follows.

2. It is directly practiced by families and society who say that

they do not allow *psychosocial-sexual expression and especially sexual intercourse by the mentally retarded*. This attitude usually means any sexual activity that involves two people, whether of the same or opposite-sex. The mentally retarded are labeled *bad* or *doing something wrong* if they engage in activities practiced by other young adults all over the world who are not labeled *mentally retarded*.

To the extent that the above is enforced, there are usually well understood consequences if rules of sexual behavior are not followed. The consequences vary from separation and counseling (which would be appropriate in some situations and not others) to punishment (which is rarely appropriate for two consenting adults who have not been adjudicated incompetent). In other cases, privileges are often held as rewards and positive reinforcement if abstinence rules are followed.

These are the atmospheres in which the staff members and administrators are most comfortable. If one of the two approaches must be taken, it is more advantageous to program the mentally retarded on a positive privilege orientated program so that the behavior modification achieved will be meaningful and will become part of the daily schema of living.

It is most important and judicious to involve the sex educator/sex counselor in communicating the psychosocial-sexual rules and limitations. This person is better trained and comfortable with talking about sexuality and sexual expression. The mentally retarded individual can be aimed toward acceptable forms of sexual expression for the specific environments. Life will become less constantly frustrating.

The problem with an approach which uses a specially trained person is that this person is usually only available when time can be scheduled. In contrast, the people who work daily with the mentally retarded individual have the most contact with the person. This makes intervention at the most judicious moments more feasible. Good counseling and intervention can be provided in a relaxed and nonspecific therapeutic atmosphere. This is why it is important for every individual, from the highest staff member to the lowest and all family members to be trained. In this way the most effective communication system will exist and the most productive outcomes will emerge.

The questions still are "Are there specific societal rules; do they exist; by whom are they determined; how are they related; how are they enforced; and do they govern the choice to live in a specific society or not?"

The answer that encompasses this group of questions is "yes," the *rules do exist; they have often been determined in archaic times; are not related to present day life styles at all; and will only be enforced in some states and by certain faction groups.*

However, because they exist, they govern the choice of the mentally retarded living in a specific society or not. Balancing this are the new regulations of Intermediate Care Facilities and the federal government's rights to privacy (see Chapter 10 regarding legal issues). Advocates and family members, along with the mentally retarded, can now choose to challenge the laws as unconstitutional. Chances are, if taken to court by a competent lawyer, the mentally retarded will stand a good chance of achieving their goal of being allowed to make the choices that are their inherent rights.

The challenge remains with the professionals, programmers, and families to help the mentally retarded recognize the need to adhere to the rules of a specific society until they can change the rules. In the meantime, the mentally retarded individual can be helped to develop the adaptive and compliant behavior required to live in less restrictive environments. This will enable the mentally retarded to have more choices about where they are going to live and function in the future.

chapter seven

DEVELOPING HEALTHY PSYCHOSOCIAL-SEXUAL ATTITUDES IN THE MENTALLY RETARDED

How can healthy psychosocial-sexual attitudes be developed in the mentally retarded? The first step in this process is making the decision that it is a necessary and appropriate area to approach programmatically. If this basic premise is lacking in the attitude of those training and teaching the mentally retarded to function and live within society, a healthy psychosocial-sexual attitude can never be communicated to the mentally retarded indvidual.

In the policies and procedures that administrators establish to provide sex education/sex counseling to the mentally retarded, it ought to be an accepted premise that the mentally retarded, as sexual human beings, go through a process of developing a psychosocial-sexual self. As such, it is possible to structure the learning process in such a way that the end result is *healthy psychosocial-sexual attitudes*. Basically, the attitude of the people providing the training and instruction should be to help the mentally retarded develop a healthy psychosocial-sexual attitude. This is an achievable goal. Without this philosophy at an administrative level, or without family support this chapter can stop right here.

It might be asked "why be concerned with psychosexual attitudes in the first place?" The answer is simple: With an effort to establish and develop healthy psychosocial-sexual attitudes, there is a decreased possibility of seeing negative and undesirable sexual behavior developing. Self esteem will be improved and general ego development will be enhanced. The mentally retarded individual will have a much better opportunity and chance at developing in a total way which will help when encountering community pressures and developing relationships.

Psychosocial-sexual attitude development should be the natural outgrowth of any competent sex education/sex counseling program that deals with feelings and development of the self. This programming should also teach the basics of body anatomy, birth control, and so forth. These are survival skills. Developing positive feelings and attitudes in a psychosocial-sexual sense will help in the enrichment of experiences.

Who is responsible for developing these attitudes? Every person who comes in contact with the mentally retarded individual from birth will influence these psychosocial-sexual feelings. Therefore, the training should be done cooperatively by parents, faculty, and staff and then jointly by the faculty and parents.

Consistency in philosophy is so very important to achieving a positive outcome. If a staff member is enhancing one area of ego development in the psychosocial-sexual area, while the family is doing the opposite, the confusion will cause anxiety, be unproductive, and, in the end, would not be considered healthy.

Example A:

In a residential facility, the staff is encouraging the mentally retarded person to masturbate in order to feel good sexually and to develop positive self-concepts in a psychosocial-sexual way. The individual goes home for a visit but is found masturbating by a family member who says that masturbation is "bad, wrong and to stop." The result is confusion and poor self-concept. The mentally retarded person is made to feel failure again along with the inability to please anyone including the self.

This process should always emphasize the positive things or skills that mentally retarded persons have that make them feel good about themselves. The feelings of maleness or femaleness and the roles that sexuality usually plays in the development of self should be explored. Why do many mentally retarded people see themselves as nonsexual? Basically because that is the way they have been viewed by parents, family, and professionals. People tend to respond as they are treated.

If the desired end result is for the mentally retarded person to feel good about emerging sexuality, then teach all of the technical aspects of sex education plus the areas of understanding of feelings that accompany these topics.

Emphasis should be focused on the fact that, because a person carries the label of being *mentally retarded*, much of society will consider that person as having no psychosocial-sexual attitudes or feelings. The mentally retarded need to be helped to understand that they do indeed have these feelings and attitudes. They should be encouraged to accept them within the scope of their environments, families, and society. Counseling should be provided to help the mentally retarded handle those aspects of their psychosocial-sexual attitudes that are weak or causing inner feelings of conflict.

This programming should be done on a very individual level. Once psychosocial-sexual attitudes are recognized as needs, engaging a competent professional would be the proper approach to take. This professional would develop a specific program for the mentally retarded person and work with that individual and the environment to make it a positive experience with appropriate gains and achievements commensurate with the mentally retarded person's ability.

The limitations of topics and subject boundaries should be the innate restrictions of the mentally retarded person's ability to adapt or learn. This should not be reflected by constraints and restraints imposed by society, family, policies, or laws that deny the existence of sexuality in the mentally retarded. If this occurred, society would never see the need to approach the area of developing healthy psychosocial-sexual attitudes in the mentally retarded population.

chapter eight

PUBLIC RELATIONS FOR SEX EDUCATION/SEX COUNSELING FOR THE MENTALLY RETARDED

To provide adequate sex education/sex counseling programs for the mentally retarded, the often adverse reactions of parents, staff, and community need to be countered with positive and effective public relations.

METHODS OF PRESENTATION

Methods of presentations can be lectures, question and answer sessions, interviews in the mass media, or dissemination of printed material that is meaningful to the audiences. When possible, workshops, where the participants will have the time and opportunity to work through their feelings and information-base in relationship to mental retardation and the component of sexuality, are effective models to use.

Videotapes showing specific examples, visual graphic displays, and when appropriate, high level mentally retarded individuals participating on a panel to express their feelings and views can be very effective. It is also good practice to involve the advocacy office or legal counselor in these presentations so that the rights, as granted by the constitution, can be presented. Having a medical person available to discuss family planning clinics and their roles with the mentally retarded, sterilization and its ramifications, birth control, and related topics, is beneficial in a group presentation.

The main goal of any public relations program would be to build comprehension of the needs, problems, and approaches to possible solutions that can be incorporated into existing programs. Information on how to begin a new program will be beneficial to the participants.

TARGETING THE AUDIENCE

If the audience is specific (e.g., all parents or extended families of the mentally retarded) an approach that emphasizes the family's role and interactions towards healthy psychosexual development would be important. If, however, the target audience is the community-at-large, the topics and subject matter should be more general. Emphasis should center basically around recognition that the mentally retarded are sexual and will behave as such, which is their innate right. In speaking of advocacy groups, current knowledge of the laws affecting sexual expression, and rights to privacy, and the relationship to someone who is mentally retarded becomes vital information.

MASS MEDIA

The mass media, including TV or radio talk shows (local or national), newspaper and magazine articles, and other written material that can be dispensed readily to the public, should be explored as avenues for dissemination. Simple, concrete terms and language should be used to explain the basic premises of sex education/sex counseling with the mentally retarded. Informing the public of the need for awareness of and recognition of the sexuality needs of the mentally retarded population is the responsibility of those professionals working in the fields of sex education/sex counseling with the mentally retarded.

Sex education/sex counseling programs for the mentally retarded should be presented in such a way that they are tasteful to the target audience. They should also be as implicit and specific as needed to communicate the information that is required.

The person providing the lecture or answering the interview questions must know the audience. For one audience, using street language as shock value and desensitization might be of a great value. However, when speaking to a very conservative group, this would be an ineffective approach to use. It would stop the communication. Nothing would be accomplished. The target audience needs to be accepted where it is and then encouraged and guided to move to another level when it is ready.

There should be a concerted effort to have the public relations information presented by someone knowledgeable and experienced in the field of mental retardation and sex education/sex counseling. There will be many questions asked, and the more experience and confidence the speaker has, the more effective the program will be.

chapter nine
GENITALLY DIRECTED SELF-STIMULATION

Self-stimulation encompasses the five different senses of vision, hearing, touching, tasting and smelling. The mentally retarded often engage in perseverative self-stimulation activities such as rocking, head banging, thumb sucking, or twirling. All of these activities appear to be done for the purpose of pleasure seeking by the individual. Not all are masturbatory or sexual in nature. Nongenitally oriented psychosexual release encompasses all aspects of adaptive behavior in a social context. This includes eating, dancing, singing, games, recreation, movies, religious nurture, and all types of interpersonal relations.

MASTURBATION

When self-stimulation focuses around and centers on the genitals, it is called *masturbation. Masturbation* is seldom seen as the end result of sexual expression. This bias is not useful when working with the mentally retarded. For, in reality, it may be that the most appropriate form of sexual expression for this population is *masturbation*. We know that the mentally retarded are going to be sexual and explore pleasurable sexual behavior — why not then direct it in a purposeful and nonguilt ridden direction?

It is often found that the moderately, severely, and profoundly mentally retarded tend to perseverate. An observational and behavioral evaluation is necessary to determine whether the *masturbation* is voluntary and purposeful towards sexual release. It may be just a perseverative primitive behavior that is pleasure seeking, with no ultimate sexual goal for the individual.

MILDLY MENTALLY RETARDED

With the mildly mentally retarded, behavioral patterns similar to the nonmentally retarded can be observed. Antisocial and problematic areas of sexual expression can be controlled in fairly traditional and available modes. However, as the level of mental retardation is lowered, cognitive and adaptive skills levels dictate that professional interactive levels must change. The professional should be able to observe and analyze the genitally directed self stimulating behavior of the mentally retarded individual and make a value judgment as to whether the mentally retarded individual is deriving satisfaction and pleasure from *masturbation* or whether this is just becoming a conditioned and self-stimulatory activity.

In the nonretarded population, *masturbation* is often a part of foreplay and/or sexual performance. In the mentally retarded population, *masturbation* can be presented as the "accepted nonharmful sexual behavior that is desirous." If this is the case, it should be taught in depth. At the very minimum, the nonretarded adult in the environment ought to be totally aware of the extent of knowledge the mentally retarded have about their bodies and about masturbatory techniques towards self-satisfaction. Knowing this will make it easier to redirect activity that appears to be perseverative and nonpurposeful in nature. Does this mean that the adult sits there, passively watching and observing the mentally retarded person masturbate to see if a climax is reached? No. It does imply that the adult will be aware of the activities of the mentally retarded individual. When these self-stimulating activities are sexual in nature, they will be accepted as such. The individual will be channelled into appropriate and nonharmful ways of masturbating. The adult should help the individual to feel good sexually in a way acceptable to the confines of the environment. Assumptions cannot be made that the mentally retarded know how to do what will feel good concerning masturbation.

Generally accepted learning avenues, such as books, erotic movies, peer learning, extended family interactions, are often not available to the mentally retarded population. If available, there might not be enough skill level to interpret and process the incoming information into meaningful and useful material to the individuals so that it can be incorporated into a daily living schema.

MODERATELY/SEVERELY MENTALLY RETARDED

What is the solution for the moderately/severely mentally retarded male who frequently has a red and raw penis from rubbing it continuously without any lubrication? It is the responsibility of the adult to teach this man that it is not appropriate to walk around with his penis hanging out of his clothing so that he can rub it whenever he wants. It is also the responsibility of the caregiving adult to impart necessary information in a way that can be understood so that when in his "private" domain this man will self-stimulate his genitals in a nonharmful way. In this case, possibly using a readily available lubricant such as soap (while in the shower) or body lotion so that self-stimulating his penis will not leave it red and raw. This information can be given in such a way that it is useable. The following conversation is an example that demonstrated this:

Sex Counselor: Steven, you are hurting your penis by rubbing it a lot and making it dry and raw. But if you put some lotion on your hand first or rub your penis with soap while you shower , it will still feel good and you won't make your penis red and raw. Why don't you try what I'm saying the next time you feel like rubbing your penis. Just remember to go to a private place because you shouldn't be playing with your penis in front of everybody else. And let me know if it hurts when you masturbate with the soap or lotion and we'll try to find something else. O.K.?

This indirect teaching method should not be uncomfortable to the adult. However, what if the level of mental retardation is severe/profound and cognitive understanding and processing is too low to decode and use the information in the above conversation? If that is the case, but the mentally retarded individual still has raw, reddened genitals, what is the responsibility of the adult? So many people feel "If I could only help them masturbate to climax, they would stop and move on to a purposeful activity, and next time, they would know how to do it themselves." Well, maybe and maybe not. If the mentally retarded individual is generally into self-stimulatory behavior, whether genitally oriented or not, it may be difficult to inhibit responses or develop incompatible responses to the behavior. This is where behavioral observation, program analysis and other techniques must be used to help assess exactly what the mentally retarded individual appears to be wanting. If the behavior is harmful or socially unacceptable, substitute behavior and/or activities need to be established, conditioned, and reinforced.

In the severely/profoundly mentally retarded population, there is a great deal of primitive pleasure seeking activity that can be perseverative in nature. When this is genitally directed, sexual release or climax may not be either a goal or a helpmate in reducing the perseveration of overt sexual behavior. Several quesitons need to be addressed: What behaviors are acceptable in the mentally retarded individual's environment and how can that person best be helped to exhibit the necessary adaptive behavior to live within that environment?

VALUE JUDGMENT

How can we be most helpful to these mentally retarded individuals so that their lives and sexual expression can be more meaningful to them and more acceptable to the environments in which they live? Whenever masturbation is explored with the mentally retarded, there are factors that should be acknowledged and understood. These include the cognitive, adaptive, and environmental restrictions surrounding the individual. These factors can act either as aids or restraints to the individual.

Not all people find masturbation an acceptable social activity. It is imperative to have society recognize that the mentally retarded do indeed have the right to masturbate, if done in an acceptable way and in the proper environmental setting. If masturbation exists to the point that it is distracting from any other training or programming, it is seen as being too egocentric. To be accepted by society, conditions must exist so that the individual cannot take advantage of other people. Masturbation will never be accepted as the only purposeful developmental activity that the mentally retarded individual engages in, hour after hour, day after day. Perseveration of masturbatory behavior, to the exclusion of all other meaningful programming, often is seen as undesirable by society and nonpurposeful to the well being of the individual.

Those dealing with the mentally retarded should understand masturbation in relationship to the different levels of mental retardation. This statement is not meant to stereotype sexual behaviors to levels of mental retardation. It is meant to help the reader understand the development of adaptive behavior and cognitive coping-skills in relationship to sexuality and the mentally retarded. These individuals should be allowed to develop appropriate methods of self-stimulation that are nonharmful.

Problems are inherent in this approach. Mentally retarded individuals have lowered adaptive and discrimination skills. Often, mentally retarded individuals do not know how to choose a masturbatory method that is nonharmful. In fact, the mentally retarded may be totally unaware that there are different ways in which to masturbate. Therefore, the mentally retarded may need help in the development of good sexual feelings about themselves. Emphasis on appropriate masturbatory techniques should be the most important point to communicate to those individuals who are mildly mentally retarded. The mildly mentally retarded population is usually verbal or has a well developed communication system through which verbal information and suggestions can be imparted and discussed.

With the moderately mentally retarded individual, simple pictures, slides, dolls, prosthetic aids, etc., may be more useful. Other commercially available materials can be effective.

A LOOK AT PROGRAMMING

Dealing with severely and profoundly mentally retarded individuals emphasizes an added responsibility of the adults involved. Adults must study the programs of the mentally retarded individual and ensure that any excessive self-stimulation is not occurring due to lack of programming or of boredom. With the severely and profoundly mentally retarded population more fundamental techniques might have to be employed. If the individual is self-stimulating or masturbating in an inappropriate environment, physically remove the person and provide an alternative activity which involves the use of both hands. This procedure will condition an incompatible response to the masturbatory activity.

An example of this would be a severely mentally retarded young male who continuously unzips his pants, removes his penis, and proceeds to rub and stroke it in public. The caregiving adult has two options. The first is to consistently remove this young man from the public place to a bathroom or his bedroom and make him remain there until he has completed masturbating and redressed. However, if this is self-pleasuring behavior that is perseverative in nature, it will be more beneficial to condition an incompatible response, such as involving the young man in an activity that requires the use of both hands to manipulate a toy or activity. This shifts the perseverative behavior of the young man to a more appropriate and acceptable activity.

With populations such as the mentally retarded autistic, where there is a great deal of perseverative and self-stimulating behavior in general, a higher incidence of prolonged masturbation might be observed. This would also be true of mentally retarded deaf/blind individuals who do not have the opportunity to receive many stimuli from the outside world.

To help the mentally retarded individual understand masturbation and how to use this activity without causing harm, adults need to emphasize the use of the individual's own hands while masturbating. The likelihood of the mentally retarded individual choosing an inappropriate object is then decreased. This would apply to the multihandicapped (cerebral palsied mentally retarded) as well as the nonphysically handicapped mentally retarded.

MASTURBATION IS A PRIVATE ACT

In developing proper attitudes and reactions to masturbation, emphasis is placed on the fact that masturbation is a private act, done by one person, in a private place. Clear definitions of any terminology should be communicated in whatever way is necessary and appropriate.

The mentally retarded young adult who has good cognitive skills can be encouraged to use fantasy, especially in the area of erotic pictures, to help in developing the desire and techniques to carry out successful masturbation without harm or involvement of others.

Example A:
A mildly mentally retarded young adult male often approached other males, asking them to participate in mutual masturbation. This usually ended in anal intercourse with the aggressive young male being the aggressive partner. He was experienced in this same-sex behavior and was able to coerce other males into being his passive partner. Once this male was given the suggestion of self-masturbation with his hand, he began to experiment.

Because he was used to having a male partner, his heterosexual mental imagery was not sufficient to make him successful in his attempts to masturbate alone, using fantasy. Therefore, it was suggested that he purchase a magazine from the drugstore which would have erotic female pictures in it. He was then advised to use the magazine in private, while self-stimulating his penis with his hands to see if a fantasy level could be developed. This did indeed work. Instead of participating in same-sex activity, which the adults in the environment found unacceptable, this mentally retarded male began to use his magazines in private. He stopped involving others in his masturbatory activity.

Concurrently, he began to exhibit more appropriate social behavior in general. He gained more control over his behavior around both males and females. Most importantly, he developed a much healthier and self-satisfied psychosocial-sexual personality. This ability to generalize and use better adaptive behavior is one of the measurements of success in helping the mentally retarded develop their individual psychosocial-sexual personalities. As this young man began to adapt and generalize his behavior in a self-satisfying way, his whole ego development increased and improved. This gradual increase in appropriate behavior appeared after nine months of weekly group sex counseling sessions, during which time there were regressions and a great deal of ambivalence shown by this man both in what he said and in his behavior.

The final test of being able to maintain appropriate and meaningful behavior is unknown and only the passing of time will be the true indicator of success and the judge of whether a sophisticated enough internal monitoring system was developed during the sex counseling sessions. At necessary intervals follow-up sessions should provide the support that will help sustain inner control for outer behavior.

Example B:
A mildly retarded young female had been very sexually active with male partners in the past. She had also experienced some same-sex foreplay and mutual masturbation. It was suggested that she should explore ways to use her own hands to stimulate her genitals and breasts. It was explained that masturbation might help her receive some of the same positive sexual feelings she had experienced previously with partners. She had to accept that she was in a living environment which had rules prohibiting sexual intercourse between two people of either the

same or opposite-sex.

Because of the high IQ level of this mentally retarded female, verbal sex counseling was used to give the information about masturbation and to help her feelings to surface. She learned to use her hand to masturbate. By using a soft teddy bear as a masturbatory aid, she also explored her own breasts and genitals in a rubbing and stimulating way. This helped her develop erotic feelings about her self-pleasuring and self-stimulating. Masturbation became a more satisfying and acceptable form of sexual expression to her. She was able to masturbate to climax. At that point in sex counseling, information about cleanliness and the use of the teddy bear was discussed. She had to learn to wash the teddy bear so that she would not be risking infection and irritation of her genitals. This learned sexual behavior also generalized to other soft objects, such as pillows.

Incidences of sexual intercourse in the restricted environment decreased. The female now had a more appropriate way to express sexuality and to feel good within the confines of her environment. Simultaneously, it was also noted that same-sex foreplay decreased in frequency.

Example C:
A mildly mentally retarded adult male who was severely physically handicapped requested that he be given a doll with which to masturbate. It was found that this man often engaged in infantile behavior exemplified by frequent temper tantrums, quickness to anger at minor teasing (especially about use of the doll), obsessional desire to be parented as a young child, overly dependent with frequent refusal to do self-help skills that had been mastered (feeding himself), and deliberate urinary incontinence. These infantile behaviors caused him to be ridiculed by other males in his living environment. The staff also ascertained that he could not physically take care of the doll regarding cleanliness or appropriate storage or retrieval from a private place. For these reasons, use of the doll as a masturbatory aid was not encouraged.

After consultation with members of this man's program team who knew his physical limitations and abilities, the following suggestion was made: It was determined that this man could get his hand to his penis and masturbate, but that he was not able to clean himself afterwards. Therefore, he could be placed in the shower with a private curtain. He could either sit in a chair or be placed on a mat on the floor. He would be left alone to masturbate. At the completion of masturbating, an attendant would help turn on the shower so that the man could clean himself and proceed with his general routine of washing.

Both the staff and client were helped to develop an acceptable alternative to the man's being able to function within the limitations of his handicap. Ridicule from other clients was reduced. This was achieved because the man was given the opportunity to explore his own sexuality in a private place. Staff felt more comfortable in the way that they were helping him express his sexuality. All adults involved felt very uncomfortable about this grown man using a small female doll. However, the adults had a much more positive response to the solution offered concerning privacy in the shower.

In working with the mentally retarded to develop feelings and techniques of appropriate masturbation, emphasis is on communicating that one is responsible for one's own body. What someone does in private is a private act. Nothing harmful should be done to one's body. There are appropriate, nonharmful ways to masturbate. Repetition is often necessary to demonstrate that masturbation is a very private act, done only in a private place, and with no one else involved. Masturbation should be presented as a self-stimulation activity.

As long as these tenets are upheld, there will be less resistance from the adults who are having difficulty dealing with their own feelings about masturbation, i.e., whether masturbation is indeed an acceptable activity and whether the mentally retarded have the need or right to masturbate. Teaching appropriate action that goes along with this self-expression is teaching the *ethic of responsibility* to the mentally retarded.

In the severely/profoundly mentally retarded individual, it is frequently the case where an adolescent continuously focuses on genitally directed self-stimulation. It does not seem to matter whether orgasm occurs or not. To the adults in the environment, it seems that the mentally retarded person has one sole desire and purpose in life and that purpose is to publicly expose and play with the genitals. No kind of intervention or interaction by the adult seems to have any effect on changing or modifying the individual's behavior to some more acceptable level.

When the adult begins to feel really helpless in changing the behavior, isolation of the mentally retarded individual occurs so that at least others will not be able to see what is happening. Does this help explain some of the behaviors observed in the back wards of our institutions? Does it help explain why some parents never take their adolescent or adult children home for visits from institutions? It may help explain why some mentally retarded people who are kept at home, are locked away in a back room, where visitors and other family members will not have to observe and interact with these behaviors that connote shame for the adult family members.

The problem is that the situation becomes self-perpetuating and self-fullfilling. Certainly it is difficult, if not impossible, for normal family life to continue in the living room when any family member, retarded or nonretarded continuously demonstrates an unacceptable social behavior. Exposing and playing with genitals in public is one such behavior. The nonmentally retarded person would not be allowed to exhibit this behavior in the living room. Therefore, why should it be any different for the mentally retarded individual. The same family social rules should apply to all members of the family.

It should be an accepted premise that the mentally retarded can learn to control and inhibit responses that are unacceptable, but it may take much longer and many different techniques before one is found that will develop necessary coping skills.

HANDS-ON TEACHING

Do we have to go as far as some propose and teach the mentally retarded to masturbate by using a "hands-on technique"? This concept has so many legal and ethical complications in relationship to law, child abuse statutes, and personal morals. Why delve there and chance making many uncomfortable and distrustful of the programming that is being done? Why not develop programs and situations in which the mentally retarded can have privacy, explore their own bodies, learn what feels good, when and where it is appropriate?

Professionals can use training techniques to condition the responses and desired behavior. This is the perfect opportunity to teach respect of self, others, privacy, and appropriate and inappropriate behavior. The responsibility to the self in sexual expression cannot be overemphasized with any population. The only difference to realize with the mentally retarded is that the programming may be teaching masturbation as the desired and ultimate sexual release mechanism for a specific person in a specific living environment. This is a different approach from saying that "everyone masturbates because it feels good. As you grow up, you will learn to have other sexual interactions that will be with another person and will feel better and more complete."

This open communication with self through masturbation may be the only available life-long avenue for the person who is mentally retarded and is not living in an environment which permits choice of partners with whom to share sexual expression. If masturbation is to be the end goal for an individual, then it is society's responsibility to help that end goal become obtainable and reachable.

PERMISSION-GIVING

The adults in the environment should be the permission-giving force that says "as long as you are in a private place, relating to your body in a nonharmful, self-stimulatory, and positive way, masturbation is all right." What has to be emphasized is that one cannot abuse or use another person, especially if they are younger or more handicapped. There has to be respect for other peoples' bodies as well as one's own. Sexual activity is a very private and personal act. When sexual expression is exhibited in a public place, the mentally retarded person is exposed to the world. It should be taught that this is unacceptable behavior.

Theoretically, the above applies more to the higher levels of mental retardation. However, as the level decreases, it will take more behavior modification control programs and analysis of environmental factors to help the person develop appropriate behaviors. It should be recognized that with the severely/ profoundly mentally retarded populations, professionals may never achieve the development of inner controls. That is all right too, as long as the behavior exhibited is acceptable to the environment and nonharmful to the individual.

One primary problem encountered is arriving at a state where the caregiving adults agree that masturbation is not only an acceptable form of sexual expression, but that it is desirable and should be encouraged. What if the professional is dealing with some who say that "Masturbation is not all right. It is against their religious beliefs. They just can't tolerate seeing the mentally retarded expose, touch, rub, or play with their genitals." When this attitude occurs in a work situation, it may be necessary to say, "Those are your personal feelings and they are fine, but in this place of work these behaviors are acceptable and will be handled nonjudgmentally. While you are dealing with these clients in this environment, you need to accept that this is their reality and they are allowed to function within the broad scope of it. As long as you work here or interact with this population, it is expected that you will deal with this behavior according to the established program, not your own personal feelings."

The situation is slightly different if the mentally retarded individual is living at home and the parents find masturbation unacceptable. In sex counseling sessions with the parents, it should be stressed that this is an appropriate way for the mentally retarded to express themselves. The adult is told to direct the behavior so that it is exhibited in a socially acceptable way. For examples, masturbation should occur in *private* not *public*, and within reasonable time frames instead of nonstop marathons which require seclusion from the remainder of the family for an extended period.

RELATING INFORMATION TO PARENTS

It is important to try and help the parents see the positives of sexual behavior instead of negatives. Most parents want very badly for their children, regardless of handicap, to have the fullest life possible. Nevertheless, it is very difficuilt for most parents of mentally retarded individuals to admit to their offsprings' becoming sexual. The parents see this factor as the beginning of endless frustration. The parents just cannot see any end that will allow the mentally retarded offspring to feel and experience those sexual experiences which the parents have found to be meaningful to them.

These parents can be helped to see that there are many different types of sexual expression. Just because their child may never experience traditional marriage and parenthood does not make them asexual beings. Instead, they are people who may discover, explore, and use their sexuality in different ways to achieve good, positive feelings about the self.

Once the parents accept these limitations and stop seeing their children as extensions of their own egos, they are in a better position to recognize the important and valuable place that sexual expression and genitally directed self-stimulation or masturbation can have in the life of their offspring. They will begin to realize that masturbation is not just a process of foreplay as they may have experienced it or as a developmental sequence in discovery of self as their other children may have experienced it. For the mentally retarded, who lives in a restricted environment, it may become the truest sexual release mechanism that exists.

There are many times that masturbation is considered socially unacceptable. One of these times involves masturbating in the wrong environment, i.e., a *public* setting. *Public* can be defined in many different ways, not always meaning in a park or public facility. Within a specific living environment, *public* places would be places where other people freely walk, and are allowed to enter without knocking. This significantly limits the meaning of *private* to a *place where the individual can either close or lock a door or partition, such as a bathroom or bedroom.* No one should enter without knocking or making their presence known first. To masturbate in front of others or anywhere other than a *private* place should be considered *public* and unacceptable.

Again, comprehending the concept of *private versus public* settings is interpreted differently in relationship to different levels of mental retardation. The mildly and moderately mentally retarded can be educated and counseled to use *private* places. The severely and profoundly mentally retarded may have to be removed from a *public* place to a more *private* place. This removal may have to be repetitive until it becomes a conditioned response. The analysis and implementation of this is the responsibility of the caregiving adults in the environment.

Before entering a sex counseling session, the counselor should be very aware of the limitations which the adults and structure of a particular environment have put on individual sexual expression — specifically concerning masturbation. Different places and different societies have different rules. Counselors should focus on discussing acceptable rules for that particular environment.

MASTURBATION THAT BECOMES HARMFUL

There are many methods of self-stimulation or masturbation that are unacceptable because they are harmful to the individual.

Example D:
Severely and profoundly mentally retarded females used pointed or dangerous objects to insert into the vagina for stimulation and, in the process, damaged tissue. Because of the low language and cognitive level of these individuals, there was

increased adult supervision to see that no harmful objects were available for masturbatory use. Included as harmful objects were the females' own sharp fingernails when exploring their genitals, which turns the motion into digging that tears and injures tissues in the genital area. This was cured by clipping the nails short and trying to condition incompatible behavior (such as having the individual play with objects that required the use of both hands).

If the female is engaged in table top activities that require manipulation of objects or toys with both of her hands, she will not have a free hand to reach for or dig her genitals in a perseverative and self-stimulative way.

An added problem occurs during menstrual cycles, especially in profoundly mentally retarded females, where it is difficult to educate or condition the female not to masturbate. The problem exists of blood being smeared during the menstrual cycle. An additional problem involves the female destroying the sanitary pad and possibly ingesting it. These behaviors can lead parents to request private physicians to do a hysterectomy for sanitary reasons.

Masturbation with inappropriate objects can be most harmful if the individual does not have the ability to discriminate what will be harmful or not harmful.

Example E:

A mildly mentally retarded young man went home from the residential facility for a visit. Upon returning to the facility, he told the nurse that he had pain in his rectal area. He was taken to a physician who examined him and ordered x-rays. It was discovered that this man had inserted four sewing machine needles into the area between his rectum and his scrotum. The needles had begun to hurt. He reported the incident to the nurse. At first no one believed him until after the medical examination when the problem was confirmed. Surgery was then performed to remove the needle fragments from the four sewing machine needles.

At this point, the staff physician, staff psychologist, and clinical counselor all decided that this individual had performed a very dangerous act. The sex counselor's immediate reaction was that the man did not mean to be dangerous, but rather, was masturbating, and very inappropriately, with objects which were harmful. During the sex counseling sessions, it surfaced that the young man did actually think that he was doing something pleasurable.

As this individual's discriminatory responses were poor, he did not know how to handle the situation. He inserted more than one needle. It was only later, with the intense pain caused by the needles breaking into fragments that he realized he had to go to the nurse and seek medical attention. The needles were inserted whole but during the course of this man's normal activity the needles internally fragmented.

In the sex counseling sessions, this man revealed feelings that he thought he was doing something that would feel good. He said that inserting the needles, even though painful, was exciting. He did not realize that he would have so much trouble from what he did. It developed that, in the past, he had also inserted Q-tips into his penis so far that they infiltrated the bladder.

Here was a young man who wanted to take care of his sexual needs by masturbation. However, no one had talked to him about the process of masturbation and that it was all right. He did not know how to properly stimulate himself. He was using very inappropriate and harmful objects. This was a person who wanted to go to a group home to live. In the sex counseling sessions, the opportunity was taken to discuss the development of appropriate and nonharmful masturbation techniques that would make him feel good sexually without injuring. It was explained that only then could a recommendation to the group home be made.

Emphasis was placed on helping this man assume responsibility for learning how to masturbate harmlessly so that he could express his sexual feelings. This was done in a verbal mode. Pictures were drawn of a flaccid and erect penis. Discussions were held as to how a male can stimulate his penis through rubbing and stroking (including the use of lubricants that might be available to him), eventually leading to ejaculation. The positive sexual feelings that he desired surfaced. He did not know how to obtain these feelings previously without harming himself. This man easily understood the techniques described and went on to experiment in the privacy of this bedroom.

In further sex counseling sessions, this man indicated that he was now able to masturbate without harming himself. The prognosis for adjustment in a less restrictive living environment seemed more probable and reasonable. This situation could have been avoided if, in a sex education program, this man had had a discussion with someone about appropriate and inappropriate ways to masturbate.

MUTUAL MASTURBATION VERSUS SELF-STIMULATION

Another topic of interest is *self-stimulation* versus *mutual masturbation,* especially in environments where sexual intercourse is against the rules, state laws, etc. The question is often asked, *"Isn't it all right to have mutual masturbation?"* Basically, the answer lies in the specific laws of the individual's residence. Some laws disallow any type of sexual intercourse on state property or between unmarried adults, but do not address mutual masturbation in consenting adults.

With self-stimulation there is no fear of pregnancy. With mutual masturbation between opposite sexes, pregnancy becomes a viable possibility, as does venereal disease. The mentally retarded need to be informed that pregnancy and VD can result from mutual masturbation. Emphasis should be placed on the fact that if the sperm enters the vagina and birth control is not used pregnancy can be a result. This information is not readily known by the mentally retarded. If mentally retarded couples make the decision to engage in mutual masturbation, they need to be aware and capable of using birth control the same as anyone who is going to have intercourse.

Self-stimulation does not violate the rights of another person's privacy. However, mutual masturbation may violate these rights, if there is one willing and one unwilling partner.

Historically, in residential facilities for the mentally retarded, it is not uncommon to find mutual masturbation with two people of the same sex. This is mainly due to availability of partners. One of the main ways to discourage same-sex activity is to encourage opposite-sex activity. Because both are considered unacceptable in many environments, it then becomes the job of the sex counselor to help the individuals establish behaviors and sexual release mechanisms that are acceptable in that specific environment.

Couples engaging in mutual same-sex masturbation can easily be counseled to self-stimulate as a private act, involving no one else.

Example F:
Two mildly mentally retarded young women living together in

a residential facility were encouraged individually and privately to self-stimulate their breasts and genitals in appropriate ways, instead of sneaking off together, climbing into each other's beds, etc.

As the level of mental retardation becomes lower, however, there must be more environmental controls and programmatic planning. The traditional verbal sex counseling will not be effective. In the lower level populations, the staff or parents have to make sure that they are helping the individuals to protect the rights of privacy of all concerned — both as individuals, whether mentally retarded or not, nonmentally retarded siblings, visitors, and others.

A very serious problem concerning mutual masturbation and oral sex needs to be addressed: In the process of exploration and sexual maturing, many young mentally retarded adults engage in oral sex. This could be a dangerous activity if the active partner has grand mal seizures. If the passive partner is a male, he could suffer a penectomy. This is a very hard concept to communicate to all levels of the mentally retarded and the staff and parents involved. For the naive reader, or one unfamiliar with the behavior patterns of the mentally retarded, this example may seem pretty far out but the actuality exists and should be considered as a possibility before it becomes a probability and possible reality.

Example G:
There was a sex counseling group of mildly and moderately mentally retarded males that was discussing this problem. They were asked "What would Jim do if Eric was giving oral sex to Jim and Eric had a grand mal seizure and bit down on Jim's penis?" The unanimous answer of this mildly mentally retarded group was "Take him to the hospital and sew it back on." There is no humor in this answer, for indeed, real damage would be done to the passive partner.

Oral sex also needs to be discussed as a frequent expression of mutual masturbation in both same-sex and opposite-sex experimentation. Stress that it usually is not harmful.

SAME-SEX MASTURBATORY BEHAVIOR

In the residential facility for the mentally retarded mutual masturbation also occurs between two or more clients of the same sex. Society often misinterprets that the mentally retarded are not sophisticated in their sexual experimentation. The following incident demonstrates that the level of sophistication and experimentation is greater than that imagined by most people.

Example H:
Three adult mildly mentally retarded males were engaging in mutual masturbation. Their sexual activity culminated in all three males having anal intercourse with each other at the same time. When this information surfaced in sex counseling, the men were urged to examine the appropriateness of the behavior they had exhibited. They were encouraged to use masturbation as a private act, done alone, and not involving others. In this incident, the males said that they were not experiencing positive feelings but were rather just having a better time than "jerking off."

The question is "What stand should professionals in that environment take?" Because these men were only mildly mentally retarded should they have been residing in a residential facility? However, because living there, were they developing social skills and behaviors that would help them adjust to the community-at-large?

In many communities, their sexual expression would have been found unacceptable if known to the *public*. Because these men all had the potential for community living, it was the responsibility of the residential staff to help them learn what behaviors would be acceptable in the community. In this case, self-masturbation was the solution suggested to the men to help them take care of their sexual needs and still be able to function within the confines of their environment.

In mentally retarded populations, and specifically in residential facilities, there appears to be a fairly high incidence of opposite-sex mutual masturbation. This often involves more than two individuals at a time. Depending on the environmental circumstances, such as whether it is shower time or free time outside, the mutual masturbation can be either same-sex or opposite-sex oriented. Often there are two or three people participating, and one individual is stationed as a look-out person. Many of these opposite-sex encounters end in vaginal intercourse. Some situations involve a person having intercourse with two or three people consecutively. Some of the male same-sex situations end in anal intercourse.

The solution to these problems are many fold and the responsibility of many different people. Supervision must be increased, especially when it is known that a client has a history of being sexually active. Birth control needs to be prescribed for people who are active sexually. Careful medical inspection for venereal disease should be available. All educational and sex counseling efforts should be made to impart information that develops inner knowledge and inner concepts which increase the probability of more appropriate and socially acceptable behavior.

In addition, self-stimulation or masturbation alone, in a private location should be encouraged. This will better ensure that sexual needs and frustrations are met.

An important, but difficult, task of the sex educator/sex counselor with the mentally retarded is to communicate the fact that self-pleasuring and good sexual feelings can be felt with masturbation. With the mildly mentally retarded, it is fairly easy to talk about feelings. It is possible to instill good self-monitoring techniques for deciding what feels good at an emotional level. This becomes more difficult with the moderately mentally retarded. It is almost impossible with the severely and profoundly mentally retarded.

Living environments for the mentally retarded often have restrictions on sexual intercourse. The avenue of education about masturbation encourages the development of healthy psychosocial-sexual development and good overall ego development.

The question is often asked, *What about the mentally retarded person who masturbates and masturbates but does not know how to climax? Look at how frustrating that is. How can we help?* At a pragmatic level, the answer has to be an emphatic "No." *Hands-on teaching* of masturbation is not an accepted practice: ethically, morally, or legally. The medical physician, within the restraints of the profession, may want to take the risk of touching the mentally retarded person in a sexually instructive way. However, the areas of ethics, malpractice, pragmatics, and appropriateness must be decided beforehand by the particular physician.

For anyone interested in this topic, the child abuse laws of the individual's place of residence need to be studied to determine at what age a mentally retarded person is still considered a child in that state. Further study of what constitutes a sexual offense, whether it be fondling, masturbation, assault (rape), or intercourse, must be explored in that state.

In many states, one will find that a sexual offense against

someone under the age of 21 is subject to punishment in court according to the child abuse laws. It is possible that a physician could not hide behind an M.D. if attempts were made to teach *hands-on masturbation* and the parents of the mentally retarded individual considered it *child abuse.* In the area of *hands-on teaching* of masturbation, it would seem that being overly cautious would be judicious.

As masturbation in the mentally retarded population is viewed, the following should be accepted: That this freedom of expression in masturbation is innately the right of the mentally retarded individual, regardless of living environment. It is the responsibility of the parents, caregivers, professionals, or other significant adults to communicate the safe and private ways in which to participate in this self-pleasuring technique of sexual expression.

chapter ten
SOCIAL CONCERNS AND THE LAW

UNDESIRABLE SEXUAL BEHAVIOR IN THE MENTALLY RETARDED

The mentally retarded population explores and participates in all avenues and aspects of sexual behavior that are seen in the nonmentally retarded population. There are incidents of undesirable sexual behavior in the mentally retarded which ought to be confronted when they occur.

The community-at-large is very suspicious of the sexual behavior of the mentally retarded because it does not expect any expression of sexuality. Therefore, the community is very upset and exaggerates any antisocial or anti-community oriented behavior — much more so than that which is tolerated with the nonmentally retarded population. The nonmentally retarded population is expected to be sexual, to experiment, and to do unusual sexual things occasionally which differ from the sexual activity of the general public. The mentally retarded are not supposed to behave in this manner. They are not supposed to have the capability to imagine how to have sexual activity beyond sexual exploration of being curious and maybe *masturbating* and having *sexual intercourse*.

The environment in which the mentally retarded live helps determine whether they experiment in certain sexual activities. The following are some fairly common areas in which the mentally retarded have trouble in the community with respect to sexuality.

Beastiality
The mentally retarded who live in rural areas and on farms are just as apt to experiment sexually with animals, such as sheep, dogs, and horses, as nonmentally retarded people living in those

environments. These animals exhibit sexual behavior towards each other and teach the mentally retarded person a lot about mating. It should not be surprising when the mentally retarded proceed to experiment with the animals, as the animals are available and usually willing partners.

In institutions for the mentally retarded, where there are horses for recreational activity, it is not unusual for a male resident to have intercourse with a horse. When this happens, the programmers have to intervene with proper sex education/sex counseling and reprogramming. However, it should be understood that if this behavior was exhibited on a rural farm, it may have gone unnoticed. Where institutional living is involved, the horse is an available partner and the mentally retarded male probably does not perceive that he will get into trouble for his behavior. The mentally retarded can be taught that sexual experimentation with animals, for the most part, is unacceptable behavior in our society.

Sodomy
Many cultures, peoples, and even state laws consider sodomy an illegal act: whether between two consenting adults, a married couple, or two single people, regardless of sexes. Therefore, it is considered by many to be undesirable sexual behavior. In reality, especially in the homosexual culture, sodomy is one of the acceptable ways of expressing sexuality.

When the mentally retarded live in large dormitories and the males are exposed primarily to males, sodomy or anal intercourse becomes a frequently practiced exploratory sexual act. It seems wise to consider this as same-sex behavior rather than homosexual behavior. It occurs more because of availability than choice and preference of partners. The mentally retarded need to be informed about the ramifications of participating in this activity in any community where it is illegal.

There will probably always be extensive arguments about whether sodomy is undesirable sexual behavior or not. Legality aside, the main problem in the mentally retarded population is the need to present proper sex education information to the males and females so that no one will be taken advantage of or forced to participate in an unwanted sexual activity. The mentally retarded have to be taught that it is all right to say "No."

Indecent Exposure
Exposing of genitals is a major problem for the mentally retarded

and leads to confrontation with the law. The mentally retarded often have the problem of not making good judgments in situations such as what to do in a public park when urination is necessary and there is no bathroom available. Such a situation is a tremendous problem for the mentally retarded person who has significantly lowered adaptive skills. Hence, a mentally retarded person may urinate openly in a park and be arrested for indecent exposure when the act was not intended to shock or excite witnesses. Careful programming will help avoid these kinds of problems for those mentally retarded who are going to live in the community.

Of course, there are mentally retarded persons, just as there are nonmentally retarded persons who receive sexual excitement when exposing themselves to helpless victims. When this occurs, the mentally retarded person should be removed from free access to the public until the appropriate way to behave in public is learned.

Child Abuse

This is an area of concern for the mentally retarded. The mentally retarded often innocently engage in such behaviors that are considered undesirable by society. All programming efforts should be made to have the mentally retarded realize what the age of majority is in the residence state. The mentally retarded must be helped to comprehend that fondling or having sexual activity with someone under this age will be considered statutory rape or child abuse, depending on the sexual actions of the mentally retarded person. Court actions and jail sentences are the consequences for this type of behavior.

Lewd and Lascivious Behavior

This type of behavior would include actions that are sexually unchaste, lack legal or moral restraints, and disregard for sexual restraints. Such behavior would also be marked by disregard for strict rules or correctness, i.e., being a "catch all" to cover whatever one does not like. It is easy to distort things in this area. If this is the understanding of lewd and lascivious behavior, the mentally retarded could often be thought to fall in this category when exhibiting behavior that goes against the moral dictates of a specific society.

So many of the laws regarding sexuality and the mentally retarded are archaic and unconstitutional. The laws do not recognize the rights to privacy for the mentally retarded. Before behavior is labeled as lewd and lascivious, all efforts should be made to ascertain whether the behavior is appropriate. The laws and restricting rules are *indeed* what are undesirable and in need of change.

Statutory Rape
Society often expects that statutory rape is a big problem area for the mentally retarded. In actuality, that does not appear to be true. The mentally retarded do have to be taught what the age of majority is. The mentally retarded should be informed that sexual activity with someone who is under this age can be considered statutory rape. However, it is not the significant problem that society would like to imply.

SUMMARY

It is important to recognize and admit that the mentally retarded will explore and exhibit all categories of sexuality — both those considered to be within the norm and those considered to be undesirable or antisocial. Being mentally retarded does not imply being asexual. Along with this knowledge comes the realization that the mentally retarded might exhibit appropriate and inappropriate sexual behavior, just as the nonmentally retarded will do. What needs to be accomplished is having society recognize the need to treat the mentally retarded the same as the nonmentally retarded and not jump to conclusions that behavior is undesirable because it was exhibited by a mentally retarded person.

SEXUALITY, LAW, AND THE MENTALLY RETARDED

Why is material about "law" needed in this book? The obvious, but not always known, reason is that there are archaic laws ruling and constricting sexuality, expression of sexuality and privacy governing those persons regarded as mentally retarded. There are numerous states that forbid marriages between people who are mentally retarded and many state statutes that remove the constitutional rights to privacy.

For those readers interested in this topic, a good place to start would be with a book such as *Sexuality, law, and the develpmentally disabled person*. The reader should proceed to the specific state laws and statutes that are in force in the state where the retarded person resides. If any change is to occur in the laws, it will have to come from the mentally retarded population and its advocates, whether it be family members, friends, protection and advocacy systems, legal aid, or whoever takes up the cause.

This section does not intend to be a legal treatise. It will only be suggested here that anyone seriously working in the field of sexuality and the mentally retarded should thoroughly ascertain from legal counsel the rules legally restricting and governing the actions of the retarded in the particular state in which they are residing. Legal counsel will know exactly where to find the appropriate statutes and interpretation that is needed for the specific situation.

The sex educator/sex counselor interested in working with the mentally retarded needs to be aware of the following for effective programming:

— Review of current laws in state where professional resides and the implications of these laws to federal laws and constitutional rights (information to be obtained through legal counsel, attorney general's office, or protection and advocacy systems, etc.)
— Conflicts in laws and how they remove innate human rights and constitutional rights to privacy
— Legalities or illegalities of laws restricting marriage in certain states
— Use of local, state, and federal court systems to achieve changes in the laws, where appropriate
— Use of protection and advocacy systems by parents, guardians, community,mental retardation advocates, and by professionals
— Awareness of legal restrictions
— Legal issues in birth control for the mentally retarded
— Legal issues in abortion for the mentally retarded
— Legal issues in sterilization for the mentally retarded
— Comprehension of due process and effective use of court systems so that procedures can be used by laymen

The sex educator/sex counselor should be aware of the above and know where to obtain appropriate and necessary advice and guidance. Thus, help will be available to lead the mentally retarded to a position where they can enjoy their full constitutional rights as citizens of the United States, regardless of their state of residence, and regardless of their level of mental retardation.

chapter eleven
INTIMACY, MARRIAGE AND PARENTHOOD

ABILITY OF THE MENTALLY RETARDED TO DEVELOP INTIMACY

Intimacy is usually conceived as a relationship in which two people share intellectual, emotional, and physical closeness. Is everyone capable of developing an intimate relationship? "No, everyone is not capable of developing an intimate relationship even though they may want to or work at it very diligently." Is a certain IQ necessary before a person has the capability to develop intimacy? This second question is answered with a definitive "No." Are the mentally retarded capable of developing intimate relationships? This third question is answered "Yes, the mentally retarded are capable of developing relationships that are intimate in all three areas of relating, i.e., physical, emotional, and intellectual." The process must be examined on an individual basis with the mentally retarded, as with the nonmentally retarded population. Generalities should not be drawn.

Again, it will be seen that the mildly and high moderately mentally retarded population will perform in this area in a way similar to the nonmentally retarded population. However, for the severely and profoundly mentally retarded, true intimate relationships, as defined above, are not readily or easily achievable.

When intimacy encompasses an intellectual or emotional support system and closeness, society and families will rarely dispute the rights and needs of the mentally retarded to participate in the relationship. However, when intimacy involves sexual intercourse, many of these same people will shy away from helping the mentally retarded develop the skills necessary to deal with the feelings, emotions, and behaviors associated with intimate sexual activity.

The stumbling block of public opinion and family acceptance needs to be overcome. At the same time, it should be the role of the sex educator/sex counselor to work with the mentally retarded individuals, alone and as a couple, to help them assume the responsibility for their intimate relationship, especially in the areas of birth control, feelings of closeness, love, sexuality, and sensuality. Through guidance and awareness of themselves and the other person involved in their relationship, the mentally retarded can be helped to have fulfilling and intimate relationships.

If the sex counselor feels that the couple is truly not capable of forming a meaningful and supportive intimate relationship, it should be the counselor's position to help the couple dissolve the relationship and move towards finding more appropriate and meaningful situations. Working with the mentally retarded who are capable of developing intimacy can enable them to develop more satisfying relationships, rather than just accepting a relationship with anyone who will respond to them. The mentally retarded can be counseled to understand that they have a choice about whether or not to develop an intimate relationship and that there are responsibilities that accompany this choice.

The sex counselor will have to work within the constraints of the environment where the mentally retarded person is living. This may involve the sex counselor helping the mentally retarded individual obtain a legal advocate to go to court and assert the right to privacy, cohabitation, and/or marriage (assuming that the individual has not been adjudicated incompetent). The sex counselor must be responsible for ascertaining the emotional, psychosocial-sexual abilities and developmental level of the mentally retarded person so that the counseling will lead the person toward a good chance for achieving some success.

If the goal of the mentally retarded individual or couple is totally unrealistic, the sex counselor has a responsibility to redirect the person or couple towards achievable goals. Often, social avenues in the community seem limited as resources for the mentally retarded to meet appropriate friends or companions with whom they might enter into a relationship. The sex counselor can uncover these resources and, through information giving, help with logistics, e.g., planning transportation to a dance or other activity. By providing information and aid, the mentally retarded can be assisted in finding other people who might share similar interests.

The sex counselor should also work with the expectations of the extended family, residential facility, or community-at-large. The extended family may support a mentally retarded couple (e.g., by having a mobile home put on the family property). This is a very different situation from the family who says they will offer no support whatsoever if the mentally retarded person moves into an intimate relationship of which they do not approve. Such action, of course, takes away the innate rights of the mentally retarded. However, it is a reality that the sex counselor must confront pragmatically if the programming and counseling is to be effective.

When such situations occur would be the appropriate time for the sex counselor to involve the legal advocate for the mentally retarded to see that innate constitutional rights are protected. The sex counselor needs to understand limitations and get legal advice when it is deemed necessary and appropriate.

Two important actions of the sex counselor when helping the mentally retarded develop the skills for intimacy are (1) to help the individual and/or couple determine what their skills are in developing and sustaining an intimate relationship and (2) to offer a support system to the mentally retarded population moving in this direction. If this is an unrealistic goal for a specific person or couple, the sex counselor can try to redirect the behavior in a way that will be appropriate for the individual and help each person reach obtainable and desirable levels of intimacy.

PARENTHOOD AND MARRIAGE AMONG THE MENTALLY RETARDED

With the severely and profoundly mentally retarded population, the subjects of parenthood and marriage will rarely have to be addressed. However, with the moderately retarded, it will occasionally be a consideration. With the mildly mentally retarded, parenthood and marriage are situations that will be encountered frequently.

When faced with the decision to support or not support a mentally retarded couple or individual in their choice to enter into marriage or parenthood, the professional has to be able to evaluate and assess the specific individual's capability to cope with the necessary and appropriate skills that will make the goal of parenthood and/or marriage an achievable one. If the determination is made that the adults involved can manage their lives in such a way that is conducive to marriage and/or parenthood, it is the responsibility of the sex educator/sex counselor to give as much support and training as is necessary to prepare the individuals for the experience. When it is ascertained that the individual or couple is not capable of functioning in the desired situation, guidance towards alternate decisions should be offered so that new and obtainable goals can be set and achieved.

Many mildly retarded individuals are capable of and desirous of entering into marriage. When marriage is contemplated, the sex educator/sex counselor should inform the couple of community resources, e.g., family planning clinics. The sex educator/sex counselor should provide the necessary education and counseling needed for developing a positive marital relationship and a responsible decision-making process about birth control and possible parenthood. The support system does not stop once the couple is married but should continue until it is ascertained that the couple can function independently.

Following are several examples of marriages among mildly mentally retarded couples:

Example A:

A mildly mentally retarded couple were married and living in a mobile home on the extended family's property. The extended family approached a residential facility to see if the couple could move, as a married unit, to the facility because the family did not feel that it was offering enough supervision and support. The residential facility did not have accommodations for married couples but arranged to have the mobile home moved to the facility where support systems were established to help the couple function in their new environment.

The couple were both given jobs and/or programming at the facility and they were encouraged to participate in the recreational activities. Someone on the staff was assigned to provide support counseling and someone else did periodic checks of the mobile home for cleanliness and safety. Arrangements were made for the couple to receive their meals in the cafeteria. The staff at the facility worked with both people as a couple, ascertaining their strengths and weaknesses. In this case, the woman was found to be the stronger of the pair. The man needed more support, which was given. The couple had tremendous difficulty separating from their extended family and eventually had to move back to their original family location.

The important thing here is that the residential facility, as an alternate living environment, was willing to accommodate the couple on the campus, without separating them or disturbing the already estalished marital relationship. This kind of openness and willingness on the part of the residential facility certainly is needed.

Example B:

A mildly retarded female had been raised most of her life in a residential facility because she was a ward of the state. Upon reaching adulthood, she met a mildly retarded male from the community. They fell in love and desired to marry. The staff at the residential facility provided counseling for the female and determined that she was capable of handling a marital relationship. The residential staff also arranged for a community based counselor to work with the male. Time was spent with the couple talking about the responsibilities of marrriage and developing the coping skills necessary to function in a marital relationship.

Once the residential staff determined that the female was capable of handling her adult life, it became the responsibility of the staff to provide the training and nuturing to prepare the female for marriage, including sex education/sex counseling before and after marriage. Because there was no extended family for the female, the residential staff acted as an extended family, helping with preparations for the wedding and participating in the wedding.

After marriage, the couple still required a support system for a while. This was provided by the community resources with back-up from the residential staff. When the couple decided to have a baby, they used community resources for prenatal care and other services.

This marriage became meaningful for both people involved. However, without the support offered by the involved professional staffs, there would have been significant problems, because the couple did not have the skills to deal with them alone.

Example C:

A couple, both of whom were mildly mentally retarded, resided in the same residential facility because they did not have family support systems stable enough to provide home environments for them. They fell in love, ran away from the facility, and got married. The residential staff tried to remain as a support system but the couple refused help and wandered from place to place, never with enough money or resources. They eventually had a baby, and were camping out or living on social welfare. When anyone from the institution would see the couple, they would report the couple looked unkempt. The couple, however, claimed that everything was all right. The baby appeared well nourished and healthy, but unstimulated and rather listless.

This couple did not have enough training in coping with new situations and survival skills to live successfully in the community. The were clinging to each other, but not approaching life in a responsible way. The baby was not receiving the stimulation that it needed. The couple refused offers of counseling and support which, of course, could not be forced on them. With proper counseling and preparation in job skills, homemaking, nutrition, and family planning, this couple would have stood a better chance at survival as a family unit. As it was, they were doing quite poorly.

There are many retarded couples who might have the desire and skills to enter into and sustain a marriage, but they do not have the skills or cognitive levels necessary to parent. For these couples, sex counseling should emphasize the positiveness of developing an intimate relationship. The couple should be counseled about the possibility that they probably will be more successful if they do not have children. These couples can be counseled to use continuous birth control, if they desire and are responsible enough to use it effectively. Where birth control is not thought to be reliable and the couple desires the marital relationship without having children, they should be counseled about the possibilities of vasectomy and/or tubal ligation. Only if the counselor achieves total comprehesive informed consent should they proceed with these sterilizaiton procedures.

Knowledge about birth control options should be made available to the mentally retarded population. Following genetic counseling, this avenue can also be used with someone who after having genetic counseling runs a high risk of producing a mentally retarded offspring and chooses sterilization. The main thrust of the sex education/sex counseling program is to inform the couple that sexual intercourse is a responsible act and if birth control protection is not used, pregnancy can result. The couple can be referred to local family planning clinics or private physicians who have experience in working with the mentally retarded. The mentally retarded should receive positive and consistent information from all people with whom they interact.

What happens to the mentally retarded couple who marries, attempts to live in the community, fails at this living arrangement, and has no extended family for support or shelter? What is the job of the residential facility at that point? Should there be group homes or community residences for married couples? Is it fair to bring the couple back to a residential facility, but separate them into male and female dormitories? Would not it be better if community services would develop resources such as supervised apartment complexes where married couples who are having trouble surviving alone could live together? Minimum supervision could be offered for the activities of daily living, whether it be budgeting, child rearing, or birth control. This seems to be the direction to look towards in the future.

All efforts should be made to keep any married mentally retarded couple together who desires it. With appropriate support systems, the probability for success in the marriage is greatly increased. Needless to say, many nonmentally retarded marriages of today would be healthier and stand a better chance of surviving, if the necessary support systems were present. This, too, is a basic ingredient necessary towards achieving happiness for the mentally retarded population.

chapter twelve
DIALOGUES AND PRAGMATICS

Parents and educators often ask, "Exactly what do I say and how do I say it?" The following are sample illustrations of dialogues about sexuality that can be used with mentally retarded young adults or nonretarded younger children. The important thing to remember is to use language that is comprehensible to the clients involved, adapting vocabulary, visual aids, and other materials to meet the specific needs of the clients.

Situation:	Sex Counseling group for five young adult mentally retarded males (mental ages of approximately ten years). All of the males are verbal but have no knowledge of the correct terminology about sexuality, genitalia, etc. (Names are fictitious.)
Sex Counselor:	Today we are going to talk about our bodies and ourselves and how we change as we grow and mature. I guess that is something that happens to all of us. Don't you agree? Can anyone in the group tell me something about yourself that is different from when you were a little boy?
Johnny:	I got hair on my face.
Sex Counselor:	That's right. As you grow up, you grow hair on different parts of your body. When you grow the hair on your face, you will begin to shave. Has this started happening to all of you?
Group:	Yes.

Sex Counselor:	Where else do you have hair that is different from when you were a little boy?
Ben:	On my thing.
Sex Counselor:	By your thing, do you mean your private area which is your penis?
Ben:	Yes.
Sex Counselor:	You are right. As you grow up, you will begin to grow hair around your penis. This is part of becoming a grown man. You will also grow hair under your arms and on your chest. Has this happened to all of you yet?
Group:	No.
Sex Counselor:	Well, it will soon. You might notice that your muscles are getting stronger too. As your body changes and matures, you will have to do different things that we can talk about.
Ken:	You mean like using deodorant?
Sex Counselor:	Right. As an adult, different parts of your body will begin to perspire, such as under your arms. In order not to have a body odor, you will want to be sure to use deodorant after each shower. Learning to keep your body clean and appearing nice is your responsibility and part of the responsibility you develop as you mature. So, let's see. We've said that everybody's body is changing some. You're growing hair around your penis, under your arms, and your chest, and face. You are beginning to shave and use deodorant, and learning the responsibilities that come with being an adult man. Do you think that it is the same for the girls that you know?
Ben:	I don't know. Is it?
Sex Counselor:	We are going to talk about how the girls change too as they grow up to become women, but let's finish talking about some

of the other changes that you men are having first.

Ken:	O.K.
Sex Counselor:	Along with your body changing, some of you may have started having some new and different feelings. I think that some of you have told me that you like girls better now and that you like kissing and touching them. So we want to do some talking about those feelings. We should also talk about appropriate and inappropriate behavior and how you are responsible for your behavior.
Jack:	I have a problem.
Sex Counselor:	O.K. Jack, let's talk about it.
Jack:	I wake up at night and it is like I have 'peed' all over the bed. I have been scared to tell Mother. So I try to hide it, but I did not even wet the bed when I was a little boy.
Sex Counselor:	You are not wetting the bed now. Most men have something called 'wet dreams.' This means that while you are asleep, something happens to your body called an erection and ejaculation. Some of you men call that 'getting hard' and 'shooting off.' When you 'shoot off' this sticky stuff comes out of your penis. It is called semen. It is not urine or 'pee' as you may call it. It is important for us to understand what semen is because it contains the sperm that can make a girl pregnant. Even though we haven't discussed that yet, we can say right now that is very important for all of you to understand what this semen is. It is just as important for you to understand what an erection and ejaculation is so that when it happens to you it will not be a frightening or unpleasant thing. When you have an erection and ejaculation in the middle of the

	night, while you are asleep, this is called a 'wet dream.' It is O.K. and normal, and it happens to most men at one time or another.
Ben:	What do I do when I have that kind of dream and the bed is messed up? I don't want anyone to see it.
Sex Counselor:	Can anyone give Ben a good suggestion on how to handle that situation himself?
Jack:	He could get a new sheet.
Sex Counselor:	Good answer. Without making a fuss about it, Ben can just go get a fresh sheet from the closet and put the messed-up one in the dirty clothes hamper. He will have taken care of the problem himself.
Ken:	Won't his mother get mad?
Sex Counselor:	I don't think so. Mothers understand what it is like when you become a man. It may be hard for her to talk about, but you can help the situation by letting her know that you have had some sex education or sex counseling. Let her know that you are comfortable talking about your body.
	As your mother and father see that you are willing to accept adult responsibilities for your body and the way it functions, they will give you more understanding and it will be easier for them to talk to you, too. Remember, not everyone is comfortable talking about sex. However, you know that I am comfortable. I will always be glad to answer any questions that you might have, as long as you come to ask me.
	Well, let's move on. We just talked a little bit about wet dreams which brought up the words erection and ejaculation. I want to make sure that you understand what these words mean. Can any one explain the word erection to me?
Ken:	Getting hard?

Sex Counselor:	O.K. Can you tell me more?
Ken:	It gets hard.
Sex Counselor:	What does 'it' mean? Remember, just like others who are around you, I will never know exactly what you are talking about and what you want to know if you don't explain exactly.
Ken:	I mean my private thing. I can't remember the word you used.
Sex Counselor:	That is fine. It may take a while for you to learn the proper words. The word is 'penis.' You may use some other words such as 'prick, dick, peter, weiner, or cock,' but the appropriate word is 'penis.'
Ken:	Yea, I knew some of those. But I heard those were dirty. I thought you would get mad at me.
Sex Counselor:	I would not get mad at you. I think that you have to realize that some of the other adults in your environment might be uncomfortable with words that are considered 'street language' such as 'dick, prick, peter, etc,' but if, by using these words, you and I are better able to understand each other, then it is fine for you to use the words in here. I would like to have all of you try to remember the proper or appropriate words too. We will work on it together. Why doesn't everyone say the word 'penis?'
Group:	Penis.
Sex Counselor:	Good. Now let's get back to Ken trying to find out more about an erection. What he was trying to tell us was that an erection was when the penis gets hard.
Jack:	The bone in it straightens up, huh?
Sex Counselor:	No, Jack, there is not a bone in the penis. There are blood vessels. The blood flows in a certain way that makes your penis get hard

when your penis receives certain stimulation. That stimulation may come from a thought you have which could be called 'fantasy,' which is something we will discuss later. This may also happen from your touching yourself. This is called 'masturbation,' which we will soon talk about. This may also happen in 'sexual intercourse,' which is what two people do when they are making love. For right now, I just want to make sure that everyone understands when I say 'erection,' that that is what I am describing as your penis gets hard.

Everybody understand? O.K. Now let's move on. When your penis has an erection, there is a chance that the white sticky stuff will come out before your penis loses its erection or gets soft again. This is called an 'ejaculation.' Have some of you heard other words for this process.

Jack:	I heard 'come.'
Ben:	How about 'finish?'
Sex Counselor:	O.K. I can tell that you have heard about some of these things before. I hope that as we talk together, you will be sure and tell me anything that you don't understand. Then we can clear it up. It is your body. You are the only one who can be responsible for it. However, you can't learn how to take care of your body until you understand how it works.

Let's review for a moment. We have now talked about the fact that you each know that the word for your private area is 'penis.' We have talked about your wet dreams. When your penis gets hard, this is called an erection, and if semen comes out, that will be an ejaculation. Ready to move on? |
| Ben: | O.K. |
| Sex Counselor: | Everybody else? We can go over it again. |

Ken:	No. Go on.
Sex Counselor:	O.K.! Let's take a minute to talk about 'masturbation.' What are some other words for 'masturbation.'
Ken:	I don't know. I have never heard that word.
Sex Counselor:	Have you ever heard 'playing with yourself, jerking off, beating off?'
Jack:	Oh, yea, we know all that!
Sex Counselor:	Well, those are just other words for 'masturbation.' I'm sure that all of you have masturbated at some time.
Ben:	Do you masturbate?

AN EXAMPLE OF HOW TO HANDLE SUCH QUESTIONS THAT ARE DIFFICULT FOR SOME ADULTS TO ANSWER

Sex Counselor:	Masturbation is normal and O.K. Most people do masturbate at some time in their lives. There are some important things to know and realize about masturbation. It is your body. You are responsible for your body and you don't want to do anything to hurt your body. You want to be sure and not masturbate with any object that will harm or hurt you. We usually think of masturbation as something you are doing to yourself that makes you feel good. We want to think of masturbation as something that is private. Usually it is done alone.
	However, when and if you are ever in a sexual relationship with another person, masturbation is something that you may do with or for another person as part of making love. Nevertheless, right now, we are talking about self-stimulation or masturbation by yourself. It is very important to understand and remember that it is O.K. and normal. Most people masturbate or

	play with themselves because it feels good. But it is a private thing. Masturbation should be done in private. People masturbate in different ways. Can some of you tell me some of the ways you have masturbated?
Ben:	I like to look at pictures of naked women while I play with myself and jerk off.
Sex Counselor:	What you are saying is that you use 'fantasy' or use a picture to help you think of something sexual, such as a naked woman, in order to get some good positive sexual feelings as you touch yourself. When you masturbate, do you have an erection and ejaculate?
Ben:	Yes. I get that sticky stuff all over me.
Sex Counselor:	Do you remember the name of the white sticky stuff?
Ben:	No, but it makes babies.
Sex Counselor:	You are right. It is called 'semen' and it has sperm which helps make babies. If you are masturbating alone, there is no problem about the sperm getting in the girl and making her pregnant. However, when we talk about pregnancy and how girls get pregnant, I want you to remember what we are saying about the sperm. Remember that any way the sperm gets near the girl's egg, it can cause a baby.
	Babies are not just made when people have sexual intercourse. They can also be made when a boy and girl are just 'playing around' and doing some things such as 'masturbation.' Because if there is an ejaculation, then the semen and sperm will be on your hands, and if you put your hand near or in the girl's vagina, then the sperm may be able to get to the egg.
Ken:	What is a vagina?

Sex Counselor:	We'll talk about the girl's body parts in a little while. Do you men feel comfortable enough about your own bodies to do some talking about the girl's body now?
Group:	Yes.
Sex Counselor:	O.K. Let us look at some of the things that are similar in boys and girls. We both start as babies and then we both grow up. As we grow and change, our bodies change. Different things happen to us, because our bodies are made differently. We have different private areas or private parts which we called 'genitals' in an earlier session. As we mature, our genitals change, becoming different as we grow. Girls do not have a penis, do they?
Jack:	No.
Sex Counselor:	Girls have an opening to their body called a vagina. Can everybody say the word vagina?
Group:	Vagina.
Sex Counselor:	Good. That is a hard word for some of us to remember. It is the appropriate word. We are going to use it here. What are some other words you have heard a girl's vagina called?
Ben:	'Pussy.'
Ken:	'Cunt.'
Jack:	'Box.'
Sex Counselor:	Right. Those may be some of the words you have heard other men or boys call a girl's private area. The proper or appropriate word is 'vagina' and we are going to use that word here. We can look at our drawing on the board and see that, whereas the boy's private area or penis mainly is outside his body, the girl's vagina leads inside her body to where she has a very special area called a uterus or womb. That is where the baby

grows and develops when she is pregnant. Under normal conditions, the baby is delivered through the vagina.

The girl also has some tubes leading from the womb to the ovaries, where the eggs are kept. Every month an egg drops into the womb through the tubes, which are called the Fallopian tubes. If some of the man's sperm gets into the vagina at this time and travels to the womb, the egg and sperm will join together and make a baby. The baby will continue to grow inside of the womb. That is why we don't want to let sperm get into the vagina, unless we want to make a baby. Does everybody know how the baby is made?

Ken: No.

Sex Counselor: Let's review that. The sperm has to get inside the womb to meet the egg. This can happen more than one way. The man can put his penis in the vagina, which is called sexual intercourse. If the couple has been masturbating, and there is sperm on the man's hand, when he puts it in the woman's vagina, the sperm might travel up to the womb and find an egg.

If you don't want to have a baby, then you have to use some kind of birth control. With birth control, the girl will not take a chance of getting pregnant. We should always realize that we are responsible for our own bodies. It is our responsibility to find out and use birth control effectively — especially if we choose to be sexually active but are not ready to have a baby. Birth control could be a later discussion for us as a group.

Right now, I would like to mention a few things that you may have heard of before. For the woman there is the birth control pill, IUD, diaphragm, or foam. For you men, there is the condom or rubber. The condom is a good form of birth control. Another thing important to know about the condom is that it will help protect the male and female against venereal disease.

You know, we just can't talk too much about your responsibility to know about your own body and how you need to be responsible if you decide to become active sexually. You do not want to make a baby when you are not in a position to take care of it.

We have gotten off the topic of how we are different as men and women. As girls grow they develop breasts. The breasts are where the milk is made that can feed the baby. As you look at our diagram, you will see that women develop breasts and men do not. Men do have nipples, which can be sensitive to touch. Both men and women get sexual feelings from touching certain parts of their bodies that are sensitive and respond to sexual thoughts and touches. Men masturbate by rubbing their penises. Girls masturbate too. They touch a sensitive area near their vagina called the clitoris and sometimes they rub their breasts or nipples.

Men and women who are making love touch each other in these sensitive areas also. This brings about good and positive sexual feelings. Everyone has sexual feelings. Learning how to respond to them in acceptable ways for the environment in which you live is important. Knowing the rules and limitations on your behavior in that environment help make everything easier for you.

Jack:

I have a problem. I want to develop friends with girls, but I don't want to touch them yet or screw around or anything.

Sex Counselor:

That is a real important point. How can we learn to be friends and enjoy each other's company without making everything a

	sexual encounter. Can some of you think of fun things to do with girls that do not involve sex?
Ben:	Going to the show.
Jack:	Taking a walk and maybe holding hands. Would that be O.K.?
Sex Counselor:	Sure, that's a good idea, especially if the girl likes to go for walks and hold hands, too.
Ken:	How do I know when I can do more with a girl — you know — learn to make love and all that?
Sex Counselor:	Well, you both have to be ready to have the experience, accept the responsibility for your actions, and live in an environment where this kind of behavior will be allowed. If you decide to make love, you have to make a decision about birth control first, unless you are in a position to take care of a baby.
Ken:	What does the word 'abortion' mean and why can't we do that?
Sex Counselor:	'Abortion' is when a woman has a doctor terminate or end a pregnancy because she has decided that she does not want to have the baby. There may be many other reasons involved in the decision for abortion. Rather than discuss that here, which I think is a very personal decision between you, your families, and doctors, I would like to repeat what your responsibilities are as you begin to act in a sexual way and discover your sexual feelings. I want to discuss again with you that it is O.K. to have sexual feelings and thoughts. We all have them. They are natural and good. We just have to be resposible for our actions. I feel that we are discussing those things together today. **(END OF DIALOGUE WITH MALES)**

To prepare your dialogue for females you could go in a reverse order, presenting the information about the female body first.

Whenever a parent, educator, or group leader feels uncomfortable with a topic area, it can be helpful to present the material from a prepared outline. This will ensure proper flow of the material and information. Dialogues about sexuality become much easier to participate in and lead once the leader has had some practice doing it.

chapter thirteen
FUTURE SHOCK OR PRESENT REALITY?

When this book was conceived, there was great trepidation writing about the sexuality of the mentally retarded, making it a worthwhile effort, and still not being offensive to *any* reader. Possibly that was not a realistic goal. Only time will tell. However, what of this chapter? What if the whole book had been written as openly and descriptively as will be endeavored here? Would the book have been accepted or would it have produced so much resistance as to become an immediate failure? The truth and reality are often very hard to face.

STREET LANGUAGE: CAN IT BE ACCEPTED?

If this book had begun "F---, F---, F---," would the reader have immediately closed the book, condemning the contents? Why can not all adults accept street language and realize that the mentally retarded know the word and meaning and use it among themselves? Does it matter how many would have continued reading? Yes, of course it does, for if the reader had not continued and gleaned information from the book, no future communication would have been possible.

For the reserved and conservative in society, street language is often uncomfortable and *ugly* to the listener. Children are made to feel that there are *bad* and *naughty* words that mean *bad* things. People who say these words are *bad people*. This is a concept that nonretarded children can cognitively abstract. They realize that using one of these *bad* or *ugly* words does not necessarily mean that they are *bad* or *ugly*. This is not automatically true among the mentally retarded who tend to be very concrete in their thought and language processes. The mentally retarded often become consumed with guilt and bad feelings about themselves, and they do not even understand why. This is not necessary.

If the adults in the environment learn to accept street language and undestand any special words that a mentally retarded group uses, then it becomes easier to introduce proper terminology and teach its use to the mentally retarded. However, this means that parents, caregivers, and professionals must learn not to react emotionally to street language. Adult inhibitions about this language, when presented to mentally retarded children, are useless and nonpurposeful. It is time now, not later, for adults to accept that the mentally retarded will acquire street language, in the same way as any other child. Unlike most children, they may not have the discrimination to know when and where to use the words. This is where sex education/sex counseling help should be given.

Is this using future shock techniques? Why cannot these techniques of desensitization and demystification be used now to release the mentally retarded from their bondage of supposedly being nonsexual? Why must the mentally retarded wait for society to recognize and respond to them? What is our responsibility?

REALISTIC APPRAISAL

Let us now take a realistic, if slightly painful look at what it means to be mentally retarded and to have sexual needs, desires,and frustrations. Everyone around you expects you not to notice sex or, worse yet, to act nonsexual. All of this because you are not as competitive on the job market or cannot live independently. Must the mentally retarded be second class citizens sexually, too? Of course not but they are! It is up to them and us to change this status. The first step in this process is recognition of the need to approach sexual fulfillment needs of the mentally retarded in the same manner as those of the nonretarded population.

The mentally retarded are finally being recognized as sexual. However, who is willing to stand and be counted as someone who will help them develop their sexuality to a point that it is a positive and enjoyable part of their lives? Why is it so threatening to professionals, parents, and society to think that the mentally retarded can realize the meaning and fulfillment of orgasm, even if they cannot read or understand words such as *coitus* or *clitoral stimulation?*

Why is society not developing techniques for teaching masturbation to the mentally retarded so that they can successfully masturbate to climax and feel good about what they are doing? If a person cannot read but can imitate, is it wrong for an older sibling, parent, or caregiver, to demonstrate masturbation and encourage the mentally retarded to try it? What of the rites of initiation to which parents formerly exposed their male sons? Why is this not done for the mentally retarded son? Does he not have the same needs too?

TOO CONSERVATIVE?

Our present status is that we are too conservative to even use a wooden or plastic penis and vagina to demonstrate normal anatomy, function, and the way the mentally retarded can interact with these body parts. Is it wrong to help the mentally retarded by using these prostheses to understand sexuality and relate it to their own bodies? We do it for the nonretarded population.

Why is it so severely criticized when we even talk of doing this kind of activity with the mentally retarded? Are we frightened of public opinion? Most of us are. Most of us are in jobs where we can not ignore public opinion even if we so want. The point to be made is "Do we want to?" If not, why not?

What about the use of surrogate partners? Very reputable sex therapists use sex therapy surrogates frequently with nonretarded individuals. Why cannot this be a good vehicle of learning for the mentally retarded? Are we so fearful of *law suits* and *informed consent* when the courts are indefinite about who is or is not adjudicated incompetent? What can be done legally to make surrogates a more feasible option? Could a program be established to give special training to sex therapy surrogates so that they are well informed about the needs and communication abilities of the mentally retarded? Then we could have a sex therapist or counselor trained in mental retardation work with the couple. Is this unethical? If so, why? It is an accepted practice in nonretarded society.

FAMILY RESPONSIBILITY: HOW FAR MUST IT GO?

Some families feel uncomfortable with sex therapy surrogates. Why cannot they assume some very deep and personal responsibility for helping the mentally retarded individual learn about sexual expression? A sibling or parent could give instuction (hands-on, if necessary) to teach about masturbation and sexual interaction. It is recognized that some would label this behavior as *INCEST or CHILD ABUSE.* If parents do not want to assume this role, but refuse to allow the professional working with their offspring this liberty, then what are the mentally retarded to do? They develop undesirable and frustrating behavior as a substitute for appropriate and satisfying sexual behavior because they just do not know how to do what to whom.

The solutions are not easy. To some, they are most uncomfortable but they are necessary. Solutions must be worked towards if the field of sexuality and the mentally retarded is to progress.

For nonretarded individuals having trouble developing sexual expression, there are books, courses, and clinics. These individuals are taught about available tools and techniques to enhance sexuality, e.g., lubricants, positions, variations, vibrators, visual erotic stimuli, and prosthetic sexual aids. Many of these things are very applicable to the mentally retarded and many of these aids could be useful and enjoyable to the mentally retarded who are also physically handicapped. However, our societal rules, judgments, and constraints restrict us and make us powerless to use these tools. Even openly talking in this way is barely tolerated — much less encouraged.

Nonmentally retarded teenagers and young adults often enter into sexual affairs and decide to cohabit without great distress or notice from family or community. Why are there not situations provided where two mentally retarded individuals who have this desire are given the support system to make it possible to have the same experience? With the proper knowledge and support, they might be successful and have fun, too, while learning to be responsible in a relationship.

Should we be so frightened of these relationships developing and being consumated, or at least explored? Our fears just encourage ignorance. If that is our goal, we are achieving it well. If our goal is to develop responsible and enjoyable sexuality, we are grossly failing, and it is time for a drastic change.

SHOULD THERE BE A CHOICE OF STERILIZATION?

It appears that part of what everyone is so fearful is that the mentally retarded couple will reproduce. Even if they have a normal offspring, they will not possess the nurturing skills to raise the child normally. If that is the case, then why not do extensive and intensive birth control training and even talk of the NOW NEVER SPOKEN WORD: STERILIZATION?

It may be appropriate for two people who can make the choice to live together, enjoy a rich sexual life, become supportive and loving companions, but know that they do not have the skills to parent.

Some willingly choose sterilization. Many nonretarded people make this choice. Why cannot the mentally retarded have professional and societal support in this direction? Once the mentally retarded decide that they want to live together, with or without marriage, there is much they can learn.

Just as society willingly supplies birth control pills and instructions, it can also be responsible for supplying the sex counseling that would help make sexual intercourse a more pleasurable and fulfilling act; together with teaching the responsibility for the act. It is true that this is more likely to happen under the guise of matrimony, but, even there, professionals hesitate to provide anything but the barest information on what sexual intercourse really entails.

DO THE MENTALLY RETARDED HAVE THE NEED AND RIGHT TO EXTENSIVE SEX COUNSELING INFORMATION?

What of passion, clitoral and penile stimulation, different positions, lubricants, methods of masturbation, alternative stimulation such as vibrators ... and oral sex? Can these topics ever be discussed along with homosexuality, incest, beastiality, and other "problem areas?" Why should society wait until there are tremendous guilt feelings about the above, and feelings of neglect and rejection have developed, before it is felt justifiable to correct the situation that these *poor, ignorant people have produced?* This is acknowledged nonsense. The average person is too leery to do anything about it in our present society. Hopefully, the enlightened time is not too far in the future.

ROLE OF PROGRAMMERS

Programs have to be very sure that they have qualified programmers who are producing appropriate instruction and counseling. The privacy and personal rights of the individual should always be respected first. The reality is that ways must be developed to help the mentally retarded person explore and feel positive about sexuality. If parents, administrators, or society feel a little or very uncomfortable — well — that might be the price that has to be paid. A high price, perhaps, but at some time it needs to become an affordable one. If not, there will just be the continuation of the *"sneak around, find out on your own"* variety of sex that is often unfulfilling and meaningless to the individual.

LAWS: WHO WILL AND CAN LEAD THE FIGHT?

Just because laws exist does not mean they are good, fair, equal, or reasonable. How are bad, discriminatory laws changed and what does society do in the meantime? Just wait? None of the discrimination in the American past would have ever changed if everyone sat around waiting for it to happen. It took activists and leaders to change things. Who are these activists who will lead the fight for the sexual rights and privileges of the mentally retarded?

The mentally retarded need an advocate who stands and says, "Why do the mentally retarded have to be sexually uninformed and frustrated all the time? The mentally retarded have the right to express their sexuality openly and freely whether in heterosexual or homosexual experiences." We, as the adults, caregivers, and professionals need to be helping in this process.

Who is willing to say that the mentally retarded need to be taught how to achieve the *"ultimate orgasm"* thus obtaining the *"ultimate happiness"* in life? Will the public and public opinion allow anyone or any group to do this? How will the legal issues interfere? Who overcomes the parents' fears?

It is easy enough to ask all of these questions and state the following: "Why not confront and make society realize what is really needed and take a stand? However, who among us can disregard community opinion? Can you? Can I? Do we really want to? Would it accomplish goals?

When will the mentally retarded be allowed and encouraged to develop sexual relationships that they can enjoy? Who will teach them how to enrich their lives without hurting themselves or others? Can we be part of this? If not, why not? If not us, then who, and when?

APPENDIX

Inservice training workshops by the author currently are available. These workshops can emphasize any of the book's content. They can also explore the development of individualized multimedia, such as videotapes, that are appropriate for specific training settings. For information regarding costs and details, contact the author directly at:

P.O. Box 1870
Summerville, South Carolina 29483

The author also has access to lists of many appropriate curricula sources. Any reader interested in this listing may contact the author directly at the above address.

THE PRAGMATICS OF COLORED CHALK: A HELPFUL VISUAL AID FOR USE IN PRESENTING DIALOGUES OR CONVERSTIONS

Often we think that anything meaningful or beneficial must include expensive audiovisual materials. For presentations on sexuality, we feel that we need models, dolls that have genitalia or that can deliver babies, or other fancy equipment. The reality is that if simple, meaningful, concrete language is used with colored chalk and a chalkboard, all the information that is necessary can be provided.

The figures illustrate this simple techinique. It is important for the reader to understand that these drawings are meant to be primitive, expressionless, and similar to body stick figures that any parent, educator, or caregiver can draw easily. In fact, it is appealing to young or retarded clients to have unsophisticated drawings, very simplistic in nature, that can be drawn by anyone in any session.

The main thing is to use the drawings to show the differences between males and females. By using colored chalk on a chalkboard or colored pencils on white paper, the adult can systematically and consistently show how anatomy, conception, and contraception occur. The choice of colors for body parts is insignificant except for the fact that *it is important to use the same color for the specified body part or function throughout all of the drawings.* The use of the same color for the same body part or function will help eliminate confusion in the learning process. Each body part or function should be shown with a different color.

Depending on the client or group, decide whether to present the male or female anatomy first. On the chalkboard, with white chalk, draw two asexual bodies similar to Drawing A. For the female, say something such as:

> We are going to pretend that this is Suzie. Let's give her long hair. She is growing into a woman now, so some changes have happened to her body. She has developed breasts (Drawing B). There is an opening between her legs called a vagina (Drawing C).
>
> Suzie is maturing and has grown some hair under her arms and around her vagina (Drawing D). Inside Suzie's body is a special place where a baby grows. It is called a womb or uterus (Drawing E) and is connected to the outside of her body through the vagina (demonstrate). There are two Fallopian tubes (Drawing F) which lead to the ovaries (Drawing G) where the eggs are.

At this point, go to the drawing of Johnny and say the following:

> Now let's see how Johnny looks different from Suzie. He has nipples but has not developed breasts (Drawing H), and I guess that we can give Johnny short hair. As Johnny has grown, his body has developed and his penis is now large (Drawing I). Sometimes it hangs down and sometimes, when he is excited and has an erection, it sticks out like this (demonstrate with a dotted line — Drawing J).
>
> Johnny also has grown some hair on different parts of his body. He has hair on his face now and he shaves. He has hair under his arms and around his penis (Drawing K).
>
> Both Johnny and Suzie have glands that are developing. The glands will give off a body odor if Johnny and Suzie are not clean and have not used deodorant. This is something that we want to talk more about later.

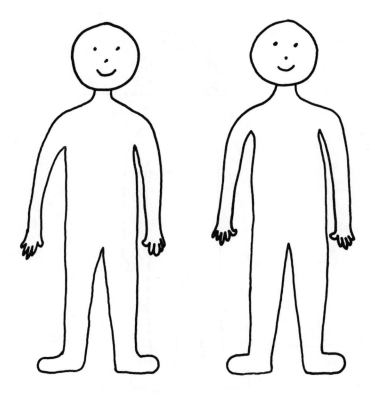

Drawing A

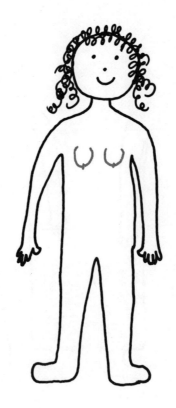

Drawing B

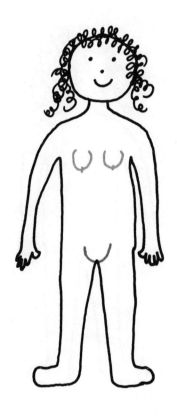

Drawing C

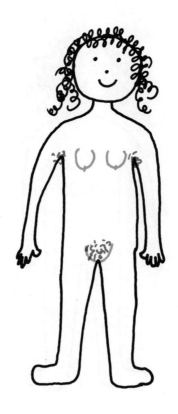

Drawing D

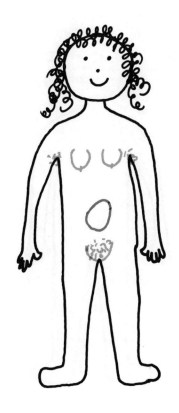

Drawing E

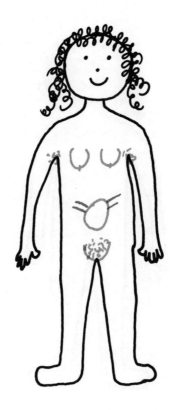

Drawing F

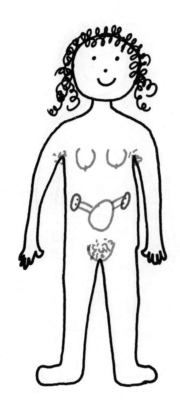

Drawing G

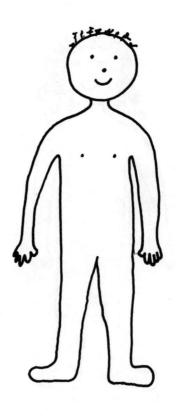

Drawing H

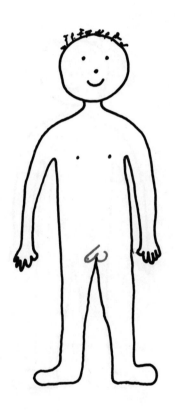

Drawing I

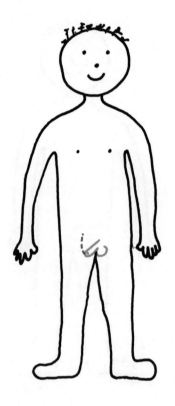

Drawing J

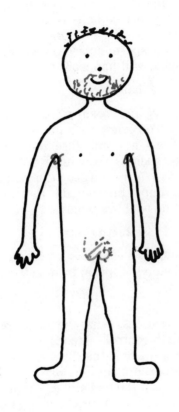

Drawing K

Now , let's continue looking at our drawings. If Johnny gets excited, a white sticky fluid comes out of the penis. The fluid is called semen and has sperm in it (draw this in white chalk). If the sperm gets inside Suzie's vagina, either by them having sexual intercourse or by it getting on Johnny's hand and then getting into the vagina, the sperm will swim up into the womb.

Remember, the eggs are in Suzie' ovaries. Once a month, one of them comes down this tube and will be waiting in the womb to make a baby. If the sperm gets to the womb at the time that the egg is there, what will happen?

Group: A baby.

You are right. The egg and sperm will join together, making a baby (Drawing L). To review, let's go to another part of the chalkboard and draw a womb (use the same colors as in previous drawings, such as Drawing E). Show by drawings, how the baby begins to form and grow (Drawing M). If we don't want to make a baby but we do want to have sexual intercourse, what do we have to do?

Group: Use birth control.

Yes. On these drawings I can show you some of the different ways that you can stop the sperm from getting to the egg and causing conception.

At this point, illustrations, using the same color system, would show how various birth control methods would work.

The emphasis being made is that by using good pragmatic and functional communication, and a box of colored chalk and chalkboard, you can keep the techniques simple and inexpensive. At the same time, you can keep your client or group interested, and impart all of the necessary information in a simple way.

It is felt that this technique would work well with any client, whether retarded, handicapped, or not. The level of language is the important factor and must and should be individualized.

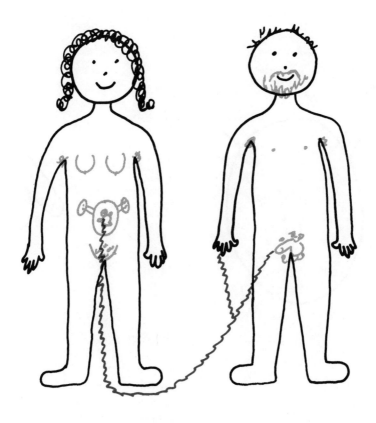

Drawing L

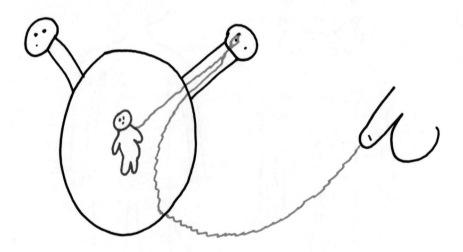

Drawing M

BIBLIOGRAPHY
and
RELATED MATERIAL

About sex. New York: Texture Films, Inc., 1972. (Film).

BARUCK, D. *New ways in sex education.* New York: Bantam Books, Inc., 1962.

The Boston Women's Health Book Collective. *Our bodies, ourselves.* New York: Simon and Schuster, 1971.

CHIPOURAS, S., CONNELUIS, D., DANIELS, S., & MAKAS, E. *Who cares? A handbook on sex eduation and counseling services for disabled people.* Baltimore: Unviersity Park Press, 1979.

COMFORT, A. (Ed.). *The joy of sex.* New York: Simon and Schuster, 1972.

COMFORT, A. *Sexual consequences of disability.* New York: George F. Stickley (distributed by Van Norstrand Reinhold), 1978.

Conception-contraception. Highland Park, IL: Perennial Education, Inc., 1973. (Film).

CRAFT, A. *Sex educational counseling of the mentally handicapped.* Baltimore: University Park Press, 1982.

CRAFT, M., & CRAFT, A. *Sex and the mentally retarded.* Boston: Routledge and Kegan Paul, Ltd., 1978.

Family planning services for disabled people: A manual for service providers. Rockville, MD: National Clearinghouse for Family Planning Information, 1980. (Manual).

Feeling good about yourself. Highland Park, IL: Perennial Education, Inc., 1980. (Manual).

FISHER, H., KRAJICEK, M., & BORTHICK, W. *Sex education for the developmentally disabled — A guide for parents, teachers, and professionals.* (2nd Rev. ed.). Baltimore: University Park Press, 1973. (Manual).

GENDEL, E. S. *Sex education of the mentally retarded child in the home.* Arlington, TX: National Association for Retarded

Children, 1968.

GIMARC, J. D. *Social/sexual living skills.* Columbia, SC: University of South Carolina Press, 1979.

GORDON S. *On being the parent of a handicapped youth.* New York: New York Association for Brain Injured Children and Its Associations for Children with Learning Disabilities, 1973. (a).

GORDON S. *The sexual adolescent, communicting with teenagers about sex.* North Scituate, MA: Duxbury Press, 1973. (b).

GORDON S. *Facts about sex for today's youth.* (Rev. Ed.). New York: Ed-U Press, 1979. (a).

GORDON S. *Girls are girls and boys are boys so what's the difference?* (Rev. ed.). New York: Ed-U Press, 1979. (b).

GORDON, S., & BILKEN, D. *Sexual rights for the people who happen to be handicapped.* New York: Ed-U Press, 1979.

GORDON, S., & DICKMAN I. *Sex education: The parents' role.* New York: Public Affairs Pamphlets, 1979.

GREENGROSS, W. *Entitled to love: The sexual and emotional needs of the handicapped.* London England: National Marriage Guidance Council, 1976.

HAAVIK, S. F., & MENNINGER, K. A., II. *Sexuality, law and the developmentally disabled person — Legal, and clinical aspects of marriage, parenthood, and sterilization.* Baltimore: Paul H. Brookes Publishing Co., 1981.

Hall, J. E. Sexuality and the mentally retarded *Human sexuality: A health practitioner's text.* Green, J. R. (Ed.). Baltimore: William's and Wilkins, 1975.

HATCHER, R., STEWART, G., STEWART, F., GUEST, F., SCHWARTZ, D., & JONES, S. *Contraceptive technology.* (10th rev. ed.). New York: Irvington Publishers, 1980.

HODGES, B. E. *How babies are born: The story of birth for children.* New York: Essanders Special Editions, 1967.

The international and domestic training and technical assistance project in disability and mental health/reproduction health care. New York: Planned Parenthood of New York City, Inc., 1979.

JOHNSON, E. W. *Love and sex in plain language.* Philadelphia: J. P. Lippincot, 1967.

JOHNSON, R., & KEMPTON, W. *Sex education and counseling of special groups: The mentally and physically handicapped, ill, and elderly.* (2nd ed.). Springfield: Charles C. Thomas, 1981.

KEMPTION, W. *Human sexuality and the mentally retarded.*

Philadelphia: Planned Parenthood of Southeastern Pennsylvania, 1972. (Film strip).

KEMPTON, W. *Sex education for persons with disabilites that hinder learning — A teacher's guide.* Philadelphia: Planned Parenthood of Southeastern Pennsylvania, 1979.

KEMPTON, W., BASS, M. S., & GORDON S. *Love, sex, and birth control for the mentally retarded — A guide for parents.* (3rd rev. ed.). Philadelphia:: Planned Parenthood Association of Southeastern Pennsylvania, 1980.

KEMPTON, W., BASS, M., & HANSON, G. *ABC's of sex education for trainable persons (THE).* Owings Mills, MD: Hallmark Films, 1972. (Film).

KEMPTON, W., BASS, M., & HANSON, G. *Fertility regulations for mentally handicapped persons.* Owings Mills, MD: Hallmark Films, 1976. (a). (Film).

KEMPTON, W., BASS, M., & HANSON G. *How and what of sex education for educable persons.* Owings Mills, MD: Hallmark Films, 1976. (b). (Film).

KEMPTON, W., BASS, M. & HANSON, G. *Sexuality and the mentally handicapped.* Santa Monica: Stanfield Film Associates, 1976. (c). (Film).

Like other people. Northfield, IL: Perennial Education, Inc., 1971. (Film).

LIPMEN, M., JACKSON, J., & STELLAS, B. *Marsha and harry.* Cambridge, MA: James Jackson, 1982. (Film).

LISKEY, N., & STEPHENS, P. *Cerebral palsy and sexuality.* Fresno, CA: Disabeled Students on Campus Organization, California State University at Fresno, c/o Handicapped Student Services, 1978.

MASTERS, W. H., & JOHNSON, V.E. *Human sexual response.* Boston: Little Brown, 1966.

MAYLA, P. *Where did i come from?* Secaucus, NJ: Lyle Stuard, Inc., 1973.

MCKEE, L., KEMPTON, W., & STIGGALL, L. *An easy guide to loving carefully for men and women.* Walnut Creek, CA: Planned Parenthood of Contra Costa, 1980.

MEYERS, R. *Like normal people.* New York: McGraw-Hill, 1978.

ORENSTEIN, I. *Where do babies come from?* Secaucus, NJ: Lyle Stuart, Inc., 1973.

PATTULLO, A. *Puberty in the girl who is retarded.* Arlington, TX:

National Association for Retraded Children, 1969.

PERSKE, R. *New directions for parents of persons who are retarded.* Nashville, TN: Abingdon Press, 1973.

Psycho-sexual development and sex education for the mentally retarded. Chapel Hill, NC: University of North Carolina Press, 1974.

RAYUER, C. *A parent's guide to sex education.* Garden City, NJ: Doubleday and Co., 1969.

REICH, M. D., & HARSHMAN, H. W. Sex education for handicapped: Reality or repression. *The Journal of Special Education,* 1971, 5:373-377

A resource guide in sex education for the mentally retarded. New York: Behavioral Publications, 1971. (Manual).

ROLETT, K. *Organizing community resources in sexuality counseling and family planning for the retarded.* Chapel Hill, NC: State Services Office, 1976. (Manual).

St. Louis Association for Retarded Citizens (producer). *On being sexual.* Santa Monica, CA: Stanfield House, 1974. (Film).

Sex education for the mentally retarded. San Leandro, CA: Alameda County Mental Retardation Service, 1969.

SILVERMAN, M., & LENZ, R. *Active partners.* Akron: Thomas Gertz and Assciates, Inc., 1979. (Film).

VARNER, N., & FREEMAN, M. *Some things about sex for both men and women.* Atlanta: Emory University, 1976

What to tell your children about sex. New York: Permabooks, 1958.

WOLFENSBERGER, W. *The principle of normalization in human services.* Toronto: National Institute of Mental Retardation, 1972.